THE DIGITAL DOLLAR REVOLUTION

REVOLUTION

How E-Currency Shapes American lives

ZCASH101

Contents

INTRODUCTION

The Dawn of E-Currency

The inception of e-currency signifies a transformation as consequential as the wandering of ancient peoples into agrarian societies, or as seminal as the clamor of industry that swept through nations with the roar of steam and iron. It is a metamorphosis that demands our undivided attention and unreserved scrutiny. At the core of this digital revolution is the Digital Dollar, which stands as both heralded harbinger and ominous omen. This currency, untethered from the physical confines of coins and banknotes, is weaving itself into the very fabric of our lives.

As we stand on the precipice, gazing into a future rife with code and currency, a profound narrative unfolds before us. The vast expanse of the digital economy opens up, promising unparalleled connectivity and efficiency. Yet, not all that shines in the servers and silicon is gold. The Digital Dollar, while poised to redefine commerce, carries with it the shadows of potential pitfalls and unforeseen ramifications.

Why then, one might ponder, are these developments laden with such trepidation? The tale is as intricate and complex as the algorithms that underpin our burgeoning virtual wallets. To comprehend this era of the Digital Dollar is to understand that it is not simply a matter of finance but of faith in what we cannot see. Currency, from its earliest incarnations, has rested on the tenets of trust and value; the digital incarnation asks no less from us, even as it strips away the tangibility once integral to its concept.

The rapid ascent of the Digital Dollar paints a portrait of a society redefining what it means to transact. Yet, beneath the veneer of its technical brilliance, there dwells a host of ramifications that gnaw at the roots of our societal constructs. Privacy, once a shield held high by individuals against the probing eyes of the world, now risks erosion under the incessant march of digital progress.

Cybersecurity, a domain that was once relegated to the esoteric realms of specialists, has now breached the common consciousness. Theft, fraud, and malicious exploits—terms that once evoked images of masked marauders—have taken on new form in the vast, unseen battlegrounds of cyberspace. The Digital Dollar stands not only as currency but also as commodity, one which is relentlessly pursued by forces benign and maleficent alike.

And what of those who, by virtue of choice or circumstance, find themselves outside the warm glow of the digital economy's embrace? The unbanked and underbanked, previously marginalized by the brick-and-mortar bastions of financial institutions, could either find new avenues of inclusion or face deeper entrenchment in economic exile.

The scaffoldings of the old financial edifices creak and groan under the weight of this digital paradigm. Traditional banking, once a monolithic presence, now scrambles to retain relevance in an age where transactions occur in the intangible ether. The labor market, a pulsating engine of American prosperity, must now recalibrate as the digital dollar proffers automation and artificial sagacity that could uplift as robustly as it displaces.

Amidst this tumultuous sea change, the role of governance and oversight stands as a beacon of order. Yet, herein lies a paradoxical challenge: How might the pillars of democracy—freedom, privacy, and autonomy—stand unblemished when the Digital Dollar introduces a new spectrum of control and surveillance capabilities?

As the Digital Dollar carves through the landscape of tradition, it parts the waters of national boundaries with ease, buoying the notion that it could become the linen upon which the map of international finance is redrawn. Economic sanctions and diplomatic maneuvers, now with a digital stringency, could redraw alliances and rekindle old conflicts under a new guise.

The consequences of this e-currency dawn are not isolated to the dominion of high finance and government policy. Its ripples lave the shores of every household, prompting a cultural reckoning with the very essence of money. How we as a society grapple with this shift will likely define how we are viewed by posterity.

To wade into the realm of the Digital Dollar is to explore the depths of human ingenuity and, simultaneously, the crevices of our collective apprehensions. As this treatise unfolds, each chapter endeavors to dissect the myriad aspects of this landscape, painting a tapestry of thought that is as extensive as the bytes that constitute our digital existence.

It is therefore our grave responsibility, as stewards of this epoch, to scrutinize the emancipation of currency from its physical constraints. We must consider the ways in which it empowers, liberates, constrains, and subjugates. We are called upon to question, to understand, and to anticipate the waterfall of consequences that may follow the ebbing tide of our current form of money.

As we embark on this journey through the pages of exploration and exposition within this volume, it is essential that we do so with both marvel and measure. For in this dawn of e-currency, we stand at the intersection of potential and peril. The Digital Dollar, while shimmering with promise, also casts long shadows that merit careful examination.

Let us then proceed with a blend of enthusiasm and circumspection, turning the leaf of history with hands both eager and steady. To the reader embarks on this expedition, may you find both enlightenment and caution in the chapters that follow. We inaugurate this discourse with full cognizance of the weight it carries for our present and the imprints it shall leave on the morrow.

References:

CHAPTER 1

Understanding the Digital Dollar

In the budding age of digital transactions, the concept of a 'digital dollar' has become a cornerstone topic for financial discussion, signifying a paradigm shift from traditional currency to its electronic counterpart. This shift, while innovative, carries with it a cautionary tale of potential economic disenfranchisement and a Pandora's box of ethical concerns. At its core, the digital dollar represents a significant change in how value is stored and exchanged, challenging the antecedent systems of physical money rooted deeply in millennia of history (Mallard et al., 2014). The incorporation of technology capable of instantaneously transferring funds and maintaining stringent records raises the spectre of obsolescence for conventional currencies but further exposes fissures in economic stability and personal privacy. The digital dollar's reliance on sophisticated networks and computer algorithms stands as a double-edged sword, wielding the capacity for streamlined efficiency whilst creating vectors for exploitation and control that resonate with biblical allegories of a society marked by the number— a symbol of immutable identity and overseen transactions (Revelations 13:17). As much as the scriptures prompt reflection on morality, the scientific community echoes similar sentiments, revealing that the switch to digital fiscal systems can deepen socioeconomic chasms and magnify disparities in access to technology, suggesting that we must tread carefully in formulating policies and societal safeguards (Goodhart, 1989; Raskin & Yermack, 2016). Consequently, understanding these dimensions of the digital dollar is paramount to discerning its extensive implications on societal constructs and the edifice of the global economy.

History and Development

The arc of history has shown a persistent march towards digitalization, and the concept of currency is no exception. The history and development of the Digital Dollar, or central bank digital currency (CBDC), has its roots intertwined with the evolution of technology and society's growing need for efficiency and innovation in financial transactions.

The earliest considerations of digital currency began surfacing in the late 20th century, notably with the rise of the internet, which provided a structure for easy data transfer.

Economists and technologists alike saw the potential for currency that could match this new information age (Kahn et al., 2005). Despite these early discussions, concrete steps toward a Digital Dollar were largely academic and speculative.

At the turn of the millennium, the concept of a sovereign digital currency began gaining traction with the advent of increasingly sophisticated financial technology (fintech). Payment platforms like PayPal showed that digital money transfers could become part of everyday life, laying the groundwork for consumer acceptance of fully digital currencies.

The seismic event in the history of digital currencies, however, was the creation of Bitcoin in 2009. While not a government-issued Digital Dollar, Bitcoin's blockchain technology demonstrated the viability of a decentralized ledger system for tracking currency - a key step towards realizing digital sovereign currencies (Nakamoto, 2008).

The following years saw a proliferation of cryptocurrencies, each vying to improve upon or offer alternatives to Bitcoin's model. Amid this backdrop, central banks began exploring how they could issue a digital form of their own fiat currencies. This exploration became more of a necessity as cryptocurrencies started to highlight the limitations of traditional currency in the digital age.

China's central bank took an early lead, starting experiments as early as 2014. This prompted other countries, and international entities like the International Monetary Fund (IMF), to consider the implications of CBDCs for global finance (Mancini-Griffoli et al., 2018).

In the United States, the concept of a Digital Dollar picked up significant interest following the unveiling of the Digital Dollar Project in 2020, which aimed to explore the potential avenues for an American CBDC. Around the same time, the COVID-19 pandemic caused unprecedented shifts in the global economy, spurring further discussions about the need for a more resilient and adaptable monetary system.

Debates surrounding digital currency also began to address the complex balance between privacy and security. The idea of an e-currency offers the potential for traceable transactions that could limit illegal activity, but also poses significant questions regarding civil liberties and the surveillance capacity of governments (Rogoff, 2016).

Federal Reserve officials and various economists have since grappled with the monetary policy implications of a Digital Dollar (Brainard, 2020). Central to this is the need for a digital currency design that would maintain financial stability, control inflation, and protect against the potential exclusion of certain groups from the digital financial system.

Research and pilot programs are ongoing, with proposals for the development of a Digital Dollar involving various technological infrastructures, including both blockchain and other distributed ledger technologies. Unlike cryptocurrencies, a CBDC would be centralized, highlighting the essential role of governance in its development.

Environmental concerns have also crept into the discourse, as the high energy consumption of some digital currencies, like Bitcoin, contrasts sharply with the need for sustainable financial practices in the face of climate change (Mora et al., 2018).

With these factors in mind, the evolution of the Digital Dollar continues to be marked by caution and deliberate progress, ensuring that the potential drawbacks are thoroughly understood and addressed. Central to this is the carefully calibrated involvement of the Federal Reserve, which must walk the line between innovation and stability.

As we look to the future, the history of the Digital Dollar is still being written. From its conceptual origins to its potential imminent implementation, it has become a focal point in conversations about efficiency, inclusion, and sovereignty in the digital age. It stands as a testament to humanity's relentless pursuit of progress—while also raising significant concerns about the evolution of economic systems in a world that grows more connected by the day.

Digital Dollar vs Traditional Currency In the transition from traditional currency to the digital dollar, one must explore the undercurrents that shape both realms. The digital dollar represents an evolutionary step in the grand narrative of currency history, one guided by the invisible hand of technology (Smith, 1776). This transition begets numerous questions, reflecting on the consequences such a shift imposes on society, its economic principles, and the foundational values of equity and privacy it has long upheld.

The traditional currency, often referred to as fiat currency, is government-issued money not backed by a physical commodity but rather by the trust and authority of the issuing government (Mishkin, 2015). It has for generations been the bedrock of economies, with material representations such as coins and notes facilitating the exchange of goods and services. Its physical nature has served as a tangible measure of value, storied in its ability to be held, divided, and used universally within a given economy.

In stark contrast, the digital dollar is not a physical entity but a digital representation of currency, promising increased efficiency and reduction of barriers in transactions. It functions through complex technological systems that allow for instant transactions and ledger updates across networks. The proliferation of these systems stands testament to a society that is continuously migrating towards intangible solutions, spurred on by advancements in fintech and a growing appetite for immediacy in economic interactions (Brynjolfsson & McAfee, 2014).

However, this evolution carries with it a constellation of newer, darker concerns. The digital dollar could potentiate a seismic shift in power dynamics, pivoting control from a dispersed model, where individuals and institutions share fiscal autonomy, to a centralized architecture that grants unprecedented oversight to central authorities and technological gatekeepers. This concentration of control can lead to scenarios where privacy becomes collateral damage in the quest for efficiency and monitoring capabilities are expanded under the guise of security and oversight (Zuboff, 2019).

Additionally, one cannot overlook the sedimentary layers of exclusion the digital dollar may deposit. Traditional currency offers accessibility to the rich and the poor alike; it is a technology universally mastered. But the digital dollar requires digital literacy and access to technology, creating a distinct divide. Those without the requisite tools or knowledge are sidelined, forming a new class of the unbanked in the digital age, contradictorily engendered by a technology purported to foster greater inclusion (Federal Reserve, 2020).

Currency has long served as a marker of sovereignty and economic independence. The digital dollar challenges this notion, as it inherently depends on global networks—often transnational in nature—that can erode the boundaries of state control. This dependence weakens the hitherto robust lines demarcating monetary policy and national economic strategies, positing the legitimacy of national fiscal sovereignty in an era of global digital infrastructures (Carney, 2020).

Furthermore, while the traditional currency is prone to wear, loss, and theft, it offers a degree of anonymity and freedom in transactions. The digital dollar, inherently traceable, casts a shadow on this freedom and raises the specter of "big brother" as transactions leave a digital footprint vulnerable to scrutiny and exploitation (Snowden, 2019). Such transparency, whilst beneficial for curtailing illicit financial flows, compromises the individual's right to privacy.

Inflation, too, is a nuanced conversation within the context of digital versus traditional currency. The traditional currency, managed by central banks through complex monetary policies, is responsive to a myriad of economic stimuli. The advent of digital dollars ushers in a new era where currency creation and destruction can be more precise, potentially offering new tools to manage inflation. However, it also raises concerns about the dilution of value and the speed at which such policies can be enacted, or mismanaged, in a fully digital scenario (Yermack, 2017).

Distrust in financial institutions, which burgeoned amid the financial crises of the early 21st century, has found some solace in the tangible reliability of paper and coin. The digital dollar, however, dispenses with this physical comfort. It asks the public to place their faith in digital systems that can seem opaque and intangible. This leap of faith is a psychological hurdle that some may find difficult to overcome, increasing skepticism and potential resistance to the digital transition.

The environmental impact, too, discerns the digital from the traditional. Paper currency and coinage, though resource-intensive to produce, constitute a one-time environmental cost. Digital currencies, conversely, demand continuous energy expenditure to maintain the network infrastructures they rely upon. This computation-heavy reality embodies a critical environmental consideration as energy sources and ecological footprints become matters of heightened concern (Nakamoto, 2008; Vranken, 2017).

The impacts of the digital dollar on social equity also beg examination. Traditional currency can circulate among different strata of society with little or no cost of transfer. The digital dollar may introduce additional layers of fees and technological intermediaries, which have the potential to marginalize the already economically disenfranchised (Zuboff, 2019).

It must be recognized, however, that the allure of the digital dollar is not without merit.

Its potential to streamline operations, reduce corruption, and enhance the distribution of financial services can't be overstated. These opportunities instantiate the promise of a more efficient and transparent financial future. Yet, they also pave the way towards a landscape liable to surveil and sequester economic freedoms under the guise of progress (Carney, 2020).

Theodicy teaches that even amidst suffering, there can be greater good. And so, as society grapples with the ethical quandaries posed by the digital dollar, it must diligently seek to balance the scales of innovation with the timeless tenets of moral responsibility, ensuring that the digital epoch reflects not just technological advancement, but enriched humanity as well (Hick, 1966).

As the tides of currency metamorphosis from tangible to digital, one must heed the weathered wisdom of history. The gales of progress may billow the sails of the digital dollar, yet it is the measured and cautious navigation that will ensure the vessel withstands the trials of time and the tumultuous seas of societal consequence.

The Technology Behind Digital Dollars

The essence of digital dollars lies in the technological fabric that weaves together the notion of value with the digital realm. To appreciate the magnitude of this concept, it's crucial to understand the technological foundation that enables digital dollars to function as a medium of exchange. At its core, the technology behind digital currency represents a melding of cryptography, distributed ledger technology (DLT), and consensus mechanisms.

One of the central elements of digital currency technology is the blockchain. Originally devised for Bitcoin (Nakamoto, 2008), blockchain is a kind of DLT that maintains a tamper-evident, decentralized ledger of transactions. Each block in the chain contains a number of transactions, and every time a new transaction is entered, it is broadcast to a network of peer nodes, which, after validation, add it to a new block on the ledger.

What differentiates digital dollars from cryptocurrencies like Bitcoin is the element of centralization. Unlike Bitcoin, which operates on a decentralized network without a central authority, digital dollars are likely to be issued by central banks. This raises critical questions about the balance between the efficiency gains from using blockchain technology and the need for some level of centralized control to implement monetary policies.

Digital dollars would rely on a consensus mechanism to validate transactions. In public blockchains like Bitcoin, this mechanism is often proof of work, which requires computational effort and energy. However, for a digital dollar, a different consensus mechanism that prioritizes speed and energy efficiency might be used, such as proof of stake.

The importance of cryptographic elements within digital currencies cannot be overstated. Cryptography secures transactions and ensures that only the owner of a digital dollar can transfer it, thus preventing fraud. The cryptographic keys — a public key visible to all and a private key kept secret — are akin to a digital signature (Chaum, 1983).

Interoperability is another pillar of the digital dollar's technology. The system must function seamlessly with existing banking and financial systems, allowing for easy conversion between digital and traditional currencies and facilitating cross-border transactions.

Privacy is a delicate issue. While blockchain's transparency helps mitigate fraudulent activity, it also raises concerns around the tracking of citizens' financial lives. Potential digital dollar solutions may utilize privacy-enhancing technologies, such as zero-knowledge proofs, to allow transaction validation without revealing details to the validators (Goldreich et al., 1986).

Integration with smart contracts allows for programmability in the digital dollar. These self-executing contracts with the terms of the agreement between buyer and seller being directly written into lines of code have potential to enable automatic payments and streamline financial processes.

The role that AI could play in the management of digital dollars should also be considered. AI could provide predictive analytics for transaction monitoring and facilitate more personalized financial services; however, these capabilities also entail certain risks related to fairness and discrimination.

Lastly, user interfaces and accessibility technologies will determine the inclusivity of digital dollars. They must be designed to be user-friendly, providing equal access to people with varying levels of technological proficiency and for those with disabilities.

While discussing the architecture of digital dollar technology, considerations beyond the technical aspects must also be made. There are socio-economic implications tied to its infrastructure, including the potential exacerbation of economic inequality. The technology should thus be scrutinized for its ability to promote inclusivity and its impact on the financial agency of individuals.

The employment of these technological tools must be done with a responsible approach, cognizant of the ethical and societal implications entailed. As we venture into this new monetary frontier, we must carry the wisdom of past financial lessons with us, ensuring a system that is robust, equitable, and in service of the common good.

In the exploration of the technological bedrock of digital dollars, it is also critical to probe how such currency would be regulated. While technology offers incredible opportunities for innovation and efficiency, it is equally adept at introducing novel vulnerabilities, calling for vigilant regulatory oversight (Goodhart, 2018).

The shift to digital dollars emphasizes the need for digital literacy and public education.

As society leans further into a digital economic landscape, understanding the technological underpinnings of our currency becomes as fundamental as reading and writing once were to economic participation.

In synthesis, the emergence of digital dollars ushers in a confluence of advanced technologies, entailing a host of considerations that range from security to social equity. The interplay between these elements will ultimately dictate not just the success of digital dollars, but also their potential to serve as a force for good or for ill in society.

CHAPTER 2

The Digital Economy

In much the same way that the ancient coins of Tyre revolutionized trade, the inception of the digital dollar has orchestrated a profound metamorphosis within the modern marketplace. As the landscape of e-commerce flourishes, bolstered by this phenomenon (Ritzer & Jurgenson, 2010), not only do merchants reap the benefits of expanded markets, but consumers also exhibit a tectonic shift in procurement behaviors, opting for the instantaneous gratification provided by the digital domain. While the Gospel reminds us that "For the love of money is the root of all of evil," in Timothy 6:10, so too could chronicling the ethos of the digital dollar illuminate the 'evils' lurking within its shadows. Research has indicated that the digital economy catalyzes an epoch of gig work, offering both freedom and uncertainty in equal measure (Kalleberg & Dunn, 2016). This sees traditional employment constructs reimagined into a dynamic and precarious gig economy. The promise and peril of this digital expanse are manifold, not only shaping commerce but also demanding a reassessment of work, worth, and prosperity in a world growing increasingly virtual. This chapter shall examine the essence of the digital economy—not as an ephemeral trend, but as a purveyor of concrete financial realities with implications as tangible as any currency once clutched in merchants' hands.

Impact on E-Commerce The advent of the digital dollar has poised itself to leave an indelible mark on the landscape of e-commerce, shaping not only the way that transactions are processed but also influencing how the economic ethos itself is being rewoven. So, let us delve into the ramifications—both overt and subtle—of this digital evolution on the e-commerce sector.

As businesses transition into the digital age, the integration of a government-sanctioned digital currency like the digital dollar is altering the fundamental transactional dynamics (Chiu & Koeppl, 2019). The expediency of digital currency transactions could, in theory, lead to an acceleration in the velocity of money, enhancing liquidity and potentially boosting consumer spending. However, beneath this facade of efficiency, there are underlying tremors of concern regarding the vulnerabilities this creates for businesses in terms of cybersecurity.

The projection of the digital dollar also brings into question the web of costs associated with e-commerce. Merchant processing fees, which once accounted for a sizable portion of the transaction costs, may potentially diminish with digital dollars bypassing traditional payment processors. Yet, this cost benefit may be offset by the expenses of conforming to new, and possibly rigorous, regulatory standards required for handling a digital currency issued by the government.

Small and medium-sized enterprises (SMEs) are likely to feel the impact of the digital dollar acutely. The capability to directly manage transactions through a digital currency could offer these businesses a gateway to a wider market, but it simultaneously introduces them to direct competition with larger, more resource-laden enterprises, potentially endangering their competitive edge (Katz, 2020).

The shift to a digital dollar might also reshape consumer expectations in e-commerce. The near-instantaneous nature of transactions with digital currencies might lead consumers to demand quicker, if not immediate, delivery of goods and services. This places pressure on businesses to upgrade their logistics and distribution systems to keep pace with the rapid transaction speeds, potentially escalating operational challenges.

Another concern is that of data collection and privacy. Digital dollars necessitate a digital footprint, which could result in substantial personal spending data aggregation. While this offers businesses unprecedented customer insights, the ethical considerations and privacy implications are vast. This has sparked debates around the extent to which businesses can or should leverage this information without infringing on individual privacy rights (Mayer-Schönberger & Ramge, 2018).

The international dimension of e-commerce also stands to be affected. The digital dollar could serve as a destabilizing factor in cross-border commerce, as nations with their own digital currencies might find themselves in a convoluted web of exchange rates and trade protocols, potentially complicating the global market ecosystem.

There is also the question of the 'unbanked' and 'underbanked'—populations that have traditionally been marginalised from mainstream financial services. While a digital dollar has the potential to include these demographics in e-commerce, it could paradoxically also widen the digital divide if not implemented with deliberate inclusivity measures. Ensuring that these individuals are not left behind as we embrace digital currency is of vital importance, for economic disparities can sow the seeds of broader societal fracturing (Mehrotra & Yetman, 2020).

As we consider the consumer side, we come to understand that trust acts as the bedrock of e-commerce. The introduction of a digital dollar represents change, and with change comes apprehension. Consumer confidence will be tested as they navigate this new form of currency, underscoring the importance of building robust security measures and educational initiatives to foster trust and facilitate a smooth transition.

Then there is the environmental impact—a critical consideration in our current era. The running of servers for blockchain and other digital-dollar supporting technologies requires substantial energy consumption. If not managed sustainably, this could negate the economic benefits and attract considerable criticism from environmentalists and conscientious consumers alike.

The consolidation of marketplaces that could ensue with the normalization of digital dollars also presents a concern. When marketplaces centralize, monopolistic behaviors can emerge, and small businesses may be marginalized. Vigilance and antitrust measures would then become more important than ever in maintaining a fair and competitive e-commerce environment.

Finally, the role of government policy cannot be overstated. As a government-issue currency, the digital dollar would fall under the purview of federal regulations that could shape the e-commerce landscape in very direct ways. Taxation, monetary policy, and the enforcement of consumer protections must adapt to handle the peculiarities presented by digital transactions with a digital dollar (Auer & Böhme, 2020).

In conclusion, while the efficiencies promised by the digital dollar are notable, the spectrum of impact on e-commerce is indeed broad. Reflecting on these varied considerations, it is clear that the intersection of digital dollars and e-commerce is at a crossroads, carrying the potential to revolutionize as well as disrupt the way commerce is conducted in the digital era.

The continued exploration of these concerns necessitates an interdisciplinary approach, drawing from economics, technology, societal studies, and environmental sciences, as we strive to balance progress with prudence.

Changes in Consumer Behavior Within the tapestry of the digital economy, consumer behavior burgeons as a critical focal point, particularly in the wake of the digital dollar's emergence. Once tethered to physical wallets and bank visits, consumers are now freed, transacting with speed that rivals light. Consider how it was written that a merchant shall balance his scales with equity (Proverbs 16:11). Similarly, a digital dollar must be measured and understood for its impact upon the scales of modern consumption.

The visibility and immediacy of digital transactions have coaxed consumers into a state of increased fiscal mindfulness. In an era where spending can transpire through a mere click or tap, the psychological distance between earning and spending narrows. A study by Chatterjee & Rose (2012) illuminated how digital platforms may amplify compulsive purchasing, given the diminished tangibility of currency and ease of access to funds.

Moreover, the digital dollar has recalibrated consumer expectations for transactional speed and convenience. The quintessential virtue of patience, once a mainstay in Proverbs 15:18, finds itself at odds with a society that prizes instant gratification. Brick-and-mortar businesses scramble to adapt, lest they be deemed antiquated relics in consumers' eyes, who are accustomed to the haste and comfort offered by digital transactions.

Amidst this digital panorama, loyalty programs find a new frontier. The digital dollar facilitates a seamless integration of rewards that can be personalized far beyond the cardboard punch cards of yesteryear. This customizability aligns well with Ecclesiastes 11:1, which speaks of casting bread upon the waters and finding it after many days. Retailers now cast digital rewards into the currents, engendering loyalty and repeat patronage.

Consumer budgeting and finance management are also reframed by the digital dollar. The ubiquity of personal finance applications, synchronizing seamlessly with digital accounts, aids individuals in aspiring towards the proverbial storehouses filled with plenty, avoiding scarcity spoken of in Proverbs 21:20. These tools empower consumers with real-time data, shifting budget culture from retrospective review to proactive financial stewardship.

Yet this transitioning terrain is not all fertile ground. The anonymity and facelessness of digital transactions may erode the interpersonal facets that once colored commerce. Scripture reminds us, "Let no debt remain outstanding, except the continuing debt to love one another" (Romans 13:8). The digital dollar threatens to supplant this human connection, automating the relational dynamics of buying and selling.

Environmental considerations similarly have a newfound stake in consumption patterns.

The digital dollar's nonphysical nature appeals to those conscientious of their ecological footprint, aligning with stewardship principles akin to 'cultivating and keeping' the garden (Genesis 2:15).

Yet, its underlying technologies consume vast quantities of energy, invoking a paradoxical narrative that implores deep scrutiny and resolution.

Consumer advocacy takes on modern armor in the age of digital currency. As mechanisms for consumer protection advance, there arises a need for wisdom, described as a defense in Ecclesiastes 7:12. Advocates now wield a digital arsenal to contest unfair practices and protect consumers from exploitation amidst the digital dollar's complex terrain.

The digital dollar also nudges consumers toward a tapestry of global goods, expanding the breadth of accessible markets. Yet, choices burgeon beyond measure, and discernment becomes paramount, echoing the words of Proverbs 14:15, "The simple believes everything, but the prudent gives thought to his steps." Consumers must navigate a maze of global products with prudence and vigilance.

With these shifts come heightened expectations of retail personalization and user experience. Just as the builder of a house gains more honor than the house itself (Hebrews 3:3), so too must developers painstakingly craft digital environments that honor the user's journey, thus molding consumer behavior to expect and demand tailored digital experiences.

Additionally, there is a swelling tide of 'buy now, pay later' services, underwritten by the digital dollar's flexibility. Scripture warns against the ensnarement of debt (Proverbs 22:7), yet consumers increasingly find themselves seduced into installment payments for immediate gratification, a behavior pattern fraught with risk for the financially unvigilant.

Consumers' approach to savings reflects another area of transition. The digital dollar's ease of access and management could lead to more disciplined saving habits, as the vigilant prosper (Proverbs 21:5). On the other hand, the ethereal nature of digital savings might trigger detachment and a decreased perception of their value, challenging traditional savings approaches.

The participation in the digital economy requires a level of digital literacy that not all consumers possess. As knowledge increases like Daniel's vision (Daniel 12:4), the gap widens between the digitally proficient and novices, catalyzing uneven participation in the benefits the digital dollar ushers in.

Rewiring these consumer behavior patterns necessitates guidance, as suggested by the wisdom of "the wise heart will be called understanding" (Proverbs 16:21). It is here that educational initiatives can play a pivotal role, molding the digital spender within the dimensions of ethics, responsibility, and foresight.

Ultimately, the digital dollar represents a profound metamorphosis in consumer behavior, a shift that is continuous and multifaceted. It requires a balance of adopting technological advancements while preserving the sage financial principles of old. Not unlike the manifold wisdom that has passed through generations, the knowledge consumers glean today from their digital transactions will echo into future economies, for better or for worse.

The Gig Economy Revolution has significantly altered the labor landscape in correlation with the expansion of digital currencies. As the tentacles of the digital dollar stretch further into the fabric of our daily transactions, they are intertwined inextricably with the rise of freelance and short-term contract work – commonly referred to as gigs. This transformation has ushered in a level of flexibility previously unseen, but it has not come without its own set of complexities and concerns.

The gig economy, spurred on by platforms such as Uber, Airbnb, and Fiverr, has exploded in popularity. Workers drawn by the allure of setting their own schedules and being their own bosses are flocking to these platforms in droves. However, with the digital dollar at play, the ramifications on how gig workers are paid, the stability of their income, and the protections they have under this new system are profound.

One apparent trend is the instability inherent to gig work. While traditional employment often provides a predictable and steady income, gig work is subject to the ebb and flow of demand. The irregularity of work can make personal budgeting – particularly in a digital dollar landscape where transactions are instantaneous and potentially less visible – a challenging endeavor (Scholz, 2017).

Furthermore, the gig economy, when run on a digital currency system, raises questions about wage security. Payments may be faster and more efficient, but they may also lack the safeguards of traditional banking. Without the proper regulatory framework, gig workers may find themselves at an increased risk of financial volatility and potential exploitation, especially if they lack understanding and control over digital wallets and transactions (De Stefano, 2016).

Despite these drawbacks, the gig economy operates symbiotically with the rise of the digital dollar by eliminating geographical barriers for both workers and employers. Remote work opportunities are thus broader and more accessible than ever before, fostering a more connected global workforce.

On the other side of the coin, the gig economy, tied to the nuances of digital currency, can sideline those unfamiliar or uncomfortable with this new form of monetary exchange. A lack of digital literacy, especially among older populations, may leave some workers disenfranchised and unable to tap into the gig market effectively (Rainie & Anderson, 2017).

Reflecting on the biblical principle of "a fair day's pay for a fair day's work," the gig economy, supplemented by digital dollars, can complicate what constitutes fair and just compensation. With instant digital transactions, the timeliness of payment is improved, yet the accountability for fair rates of pay and transparency of transaction records becomes a pressing concern.

The gig economy also emphasizes individual responsibility—and with the digital dollar, that extends to financial management and tax obligations. Workers must navigate a complex web of self-employment taxes, often across different platforms and without straightforward guidance.

Critically, the digital dollar exposes gig economy workers to a higher risk of financial fraud and cybercrime. The freelancer's need to safeguard sensitive financial data becomes paramount, perhaps even overwhelming, given the general lack of security resources at their disposal when compared to larger institutions (Tinagli, 2019).

Additionally, the independence of gig work, paired with the anonymity potential of digital currencies, presents challenges for regulatory bodies trying to ensure fair labor practices and prevent money laundering and other illicit activities.

Amidst these challenges, the gig economy is indeed thriving under the digital dollar's umbrella. It has proven to be a crucible for innovation, with digital payments streamlining processes and reducing transactional overheads for small-scale entrepreneurs and independent contractors alike.

However, this shift toward digitization of the economy has implications for traditional employment roles. There is potential for a broad movement away from salaried positions to contingent work, and current labor laws may struggle to adapt to this new reality. The balance between regulation and the freedom inherent in gig work is delicate and remains a hotly debated topic (De Stefano, 2016).

Perhaps one of the most telling impacts of the gig economy, underpinned by digital currency, is on societal structures. Traditional careers often come with benefits like healthcare, retirement plans, and unemployment insurance – usually not afforded to gig workers. Society must contemplate how to evolve social safety nets to account for this new class of workers operating within the digital dollar space (Scholz, 2017).

In closing, the connection between the gig economy and the digital dollar is more than just a stipulation of payment – it is reshaping our very notions of employment, compensation, and financial stability. As this landscape continues to evolve, so too must our frameworks for understanding and legislating these novel economic dynamics to safeguard those who dwell within the gig economy's borderless digital horizon.

CHAPTER 3

Financial Inclusion and Exclusion

The march into the digital age has heralded a modern era of commerce, where convenience and speed overshadow the rumble of coin and the rustle of banknote. Yet, the digital dollar, for all its promise, casts a long shadow on financial inclusion. Its ascent propels the well-connected forward, leaving in its wake those tethered to the analog financial moorings. As E-currency redefines wealth's thresholds, the unbanked—those without traditional financial services—stand before a widening chasm of exclusion, despite pioneering efforts to breach the divide (Cull et al., 2014). The paradoxical outcome harbors the potential for engendering greater inequality, as the fruits of this economic revolution are reaped unequally, polarizing society into the financially fluent and the marginalized (Demirgüç-Kunt et al., 2018). While the scriptures teach that the love of money is the root of all kinds of evil, one can't ignore the earthly implications of digital currencies, potentially institutionalizing financial neglect among the poorest (1 Timothy 6:10). To shelter the vulnerable, protective measures must be enacted, lest the least of these, our brethren, be forsaken in this seismic shift toward a cashless paradigm

(Cámara & Tuesta, 2014). This chapter contends with the dichotomy presented by digital dollars: the promise of inclusive banking and the looming specter of amplified societal divisions, questioning whether technology's advance heralds true progression or regressive exclusion.

Breaking Barriers to Banking The introduction of the Digital Dollar has ushered in a transformative era in finance, one that carries the promise of erasing age-old barriers to banking for countless individuals. Leveraging the pervasive nature of digital technology, the Digital Dollar aims to streamline monetary transactions and make banking more accessible to those historically marginalized by traditional financial systems. In discussing the potential and the challenges of this innovation, we must examine both its capacity to democratize finance and the hurdles that may undermine this democratic potential.

In the wave of a digitized financial landscape, numerous individuals who lacked access to banking services due to geographic isolation, lack of resources, or credit invisibility can find a lifeline through the Digital Dollar. By substituting the need for physical bank branches with digital wallets and mobile applications, the doors to financial participation swing wide open (Makhlouf & Hughes, 2021). The elimination of spatial constraints means that even those in remote or underserved areas can partake in the economy without the burden of travel or the necessity of proximity to financial institutions.

The reduction in operational costs for the Digital Dollar, as compared to traditional currency management, can translate into lower fees for users. As banks are relieved from the financial demands of maintaining extensive brick-and-mortar presences, these savings can be passed on to consumers. Consequently, people who might have been discouraged by high fees have the opportunity to engage in the banking system more economically (Berger et al., 2019).

However, such inclusive prospects are not without their impediments. Technological illiteracy and lack of internet access remain formidable barriers. While the Digital Dollar aims to be inclusive, those who cannot navigate digital platforms, or who do not have stable internet connectivity, can still find themselves excluded. This digital divide remains a stark reality for many, particularly in impoverished or rural communities, and it calls for dedicated strategies to ensure that these populations are not left behind (Makhlouf & Hughes, 2021).

The promise of the Digital Dollar is somewhat moderated by the necessary digital infrastructure required to support it. Governments and institutions must invest in widespread, affordable internet access and education initiatives to foster digital literacy among the populace. Without targeted interventions to bridge this digital chasm, the Digital Dollar may inadvertently perpetuate exclusion rather than fostering inclusion.

Cybersecurity concerns also permeate the Digital Dollar ecosystem, impacting consumer confidence. While the technology underlying the Digital Dollar, such as blockchain, provides robust security features, the risk of cyber theft and hacking remains a legitimate concern for users, particularly for those less versed in secure digital practices (Berger et al., 2019).

To effectively assuage these fears, comprehensive and approachable consumer education on digital security practices becomes paramount. Bolstering individuals' capabilities to safeguard their digital assets can alleviate apprehensions and encourage broader adoption of the Digital Dollar as a secure and reliable medium of exchange.

Identity verification and documentation prerequisites can also pose substantial barriers to access. The processes for establishing a digital wallet or account often necessitate government-issued IDs or other forms of identification that may not be readily available to all. Immigrants, refugees, and certain marginalized groups often find themselves entangled in these bureaucratic webs, struggling to obtain the necessary credentials to engage with the Digital Dollar (Makhlouf & Hughes, 2021).

To navigate around these obstacles, alternative identification verification methods may be necessary. The application of emerging technologies, such as biometrics or blockchain-based identity systems, offers the potential for secure, decentralized verification methods that can bypass traditional documentation requirements.

The transparency afforded by the Digital Dollar holds the potential to drive forward financial equity, presenting opportunities to track and address disparities in a more granular manner. Financial technologies can utilize this transparency in conjunction with innovative credit scoring algorithms that extend credit opportunities to those with nontraditional or nonexistent credit histories.

Yet, this transparency raises its own concerns, as the precise digital tracing of transactions can come into conflict with the privacy rights of individuals. Herein lies a delicate balance: leveraging the benefits of a transparent digital currency while ensuring robust privacy protections. This intersection requires thoughtful regulation and privacy-preserving technologies to engender trust and facilitate inclusive participation in the digital economy.

The characteristic of programmability in the Digital Dollar heralds the possibility of expanding financial inclusion beyond mere access. Programmable money can facilitate conditional transactions, such as releasing funds when a student attends class or an individual meets certain healthcare milestones. These features can tailor financial solutions to the diverse needs of users, potentially fostering greater economic empowerment and societal benefits (Berger et al., 2019).

Encouraging financial inclusion necessitates tackling not just the technological and infrastructural barriers, but also socio-cultural ones. Skepticism towards financial institutions, bred from a history of exploitative practices, can persist as a deterrent to embracing innovative financial mediums like the Digital Dollar. Overcoming these societal barriers involves a prolonged effort of community engagement, transparent practices, and demonstrable enhancements to well-being.

In summary, as the Digital Dollar strives to dismantle longstanding barriers to banking, its true test lies in actualizing the inclusive vision it heralds. This necessitates a holistic approach — enhancing digital literacy, expanding internet access, strengthening cybersecurity, simplifying identity verification, and aligning programmability with social objectives — is fundamental to ensuring that the Digital Dollar achieves financial inclusion for all strata of society.

To this end, research and practical implementation strategies must continue in lockstep, guided by an ethos that prioritizes accessibility, security, and fairness over mere efficiency or profit. As we look to the future, the Digital Dollar's capacity to break barriers to banking hinges on the collective action of governments, private industry, and civil society to address the multifaceted nature of financial exclusion.

The Potential for Greater Inequality As we delve into the promises of a digital dollar, it's imperative to confront the elephant in the room: the potential for heightened inequality. The transition towards a digital currency comes with the promise of increased convenience and efficiency, but it may inadvertently exacerbate disparities among different social strata. In this section, we will explore the mechanisms by which a digital dollar could widen the socioeconomic divide, using insights from past financial innovations as a guide.

The introduction of the digital dollar is not occurring in a vacuum; it is entering an already stratified society. The ways in which technology is accessed and utilized are not uniform across populations. For instance, lower income individuals often face barriers such as limited access to internet connectivity, which hinders their full participation in a digital economy (Henderson et al., 2018). Existing inequities can be magnified when new systems do not take into account the differing circumstances among users.

The capital required to upgrade infrastructure to support a digital dollar could also create a divide. Businesses in affluent areas are likely to adapt quickly, investing in new technologies to accept digital currency. But in less wealthy districts, small businesses might struggle with the costs associated with these advancements, potentially losing customers to more digitally-equipped competitors (Liu & Tsyvinski, 2021).

The nature of the technology that underpins digital currency could also play a role in broadening the gap. Blockchain, for example, which is often associated with digital currencies, requires a level of comprehension that may be beyond the reach of those without technical education, placing them at an inherent disadvantage (Diedrich, 2020). The biblical principle of 'to everyone who has, more will be given', seems eerily relevant, intimating a future where the tech-savvy become wealthier while the less knowledgeable fall further behind.

Financial literacy becomes even more crucial with the introduction of digital dollars.

While traditional currency can be relatively straightforward to use, digital currency systems often call for a deeper understanding of digital wallets, encryption, and the concept of digital ownership. Those lacking this expertise are at risk of being left on the fringes of the financial system.

Another concern is the participation of vulnerable populations in a system that relies on digital identity verification. The unbanked and underbanked, who often face various forms of exclusion, might find it difficult to establish the digital identity required to use digital dollars. This technology-driven economy could lead to a "new poverty" associated not with lack of money but with the inability to participate in digital transactions (Pew Research Center, 2021).

Inequality may also manifest in how digital currency impacts savings and investments. Digital transactions can facilitate micro-investing and savings in ways paper money cannot, but this assumes that users have the excess income to invest and save. For those living paycheck to paycheck, the opportunities presented by digital dollars might be irrelevant, leaving them behind as others amass digital wealth.

Furthermore, while digital dollars offer potential for innovation in personal finance, they also introduce novel vulnerabilities. Cybersecurity risks disproportionately affect those who lack the resources to secure their digital assets. The ramifications of a security breach can be far more severe for individuals without a safety net, rendering them financially and personally exposed.

Moreover, the digital dollar may influence social welfare and government assistance programs. These programs could become more efficient with targeted digital disbursements, but they might also become more restrictive. As transactions become more traceable, there could be increased scrutiny and limitations on how recipients use their benefits, curtailing the autonomy of the most vulnerable in society.

The digital dollar could also complicate taxation issues. As transactions theoretically become more transparent with digital currency, the tax system might become more progressive, targeting wealth more effectively. However, the reality is likely to be complex—digital currencies can also facilitate tax evasion through obfuscation and use of decentralized networks.

Against the backdrop of these potential inequities, it's important to remember that the digital dollar does not have to deepen divides. Regulations and policies are indispensable tools in mitigating risks and promoting equality. Strategic interventions, such as subsidizing internet access or providing digital literacy education, can reduce barriers to entry for the disadvantaged.

Historically, financial innovations have often led to periods of adjustment where inequality can grow before benefits are more broadly distributed. As society grapples with the digital dollar, proactive measures are required to ensure that this new financial landscape promotes inclusivity rather than disparity.

A conscious effort must be made to anchor the digital dollar within a framework of equity. By designing systems that accommodate a wide spectrum of needs and technological capabilities, we can develop a digital economy that builds bridges rather than walls, offering prosperity and financial empowerment to all. The scientific literature makes it clear: preparation, education, and thoughtful policy are key to achieving this balance (Liu & Tsyvinski, 2021).

In conclusion, while the potential exists for a digital dollar to create greater financial inclusion, it is equally likely to exacerbate existing inequalities if not managed carefully. As the discourse on digital currency continues, all stakeholders must keep in mind that technological progress must go hand in hand with societal and ethical progress to foster an equitable future for all members of society.

Protecting the Unbanked In the transformative era of the digital dollar, considerations extend beyond the technological advancements that facilitate online transactions and touch upon the social responsibilities we hold towards those on society's margins. The 'unbanked'— individuals without access to traditional banking services—represent a demographic whose needs might be eclipsed in the rush to digitize currency. How we protect these vulnerable populations in the wake of a digitized economy speaks volumes about the collective values ingrained within our society.

The concept of the unbanked is not new, yet their plight takes on a new dimension in the context of a digital dollar. In a time where physical currency becomes less prevalent, those without bank accounts may find themselves further marginalized. Traditional financial institutions often set barriers that make it difficult for low-income individuals to open and maintain accounts, such as minimum balance requirements and overdraft fees (FDIC, 2021).

These hurdles stand as modern-day walls of Jericho, keeping the needed refuge of financial stability out of reach for many.

Consideration of the unbanked presents a twofold challenge: ensuring they have access to the digital dollar and protecting them from the vulnerabilities that an entirely digital system can introduce. The first challenge is akin to laying down the foundations of financial inclusion.

Scripture emphasizes the duty of care towards the neighbor in need (Luke 10:29-37). Translating this principle into policy involves creating mechanisms by which unbanked individuals can access and use digital currency without prohibitive costs or requirements.

Innovation is essential in crafting these mechanisms. Mobile banking and fintech innovations offer promising avenues for inclusive financial services. However, the digital divide remains a stark reality; access to necessary technology is not universal. The unbanked are often synonymous with the under-connected, lacking in reliable internet access or even basic computing tools (World Bank, 2020). An equitable transition to a digital dollar demands significant investment in bridging this digital divide.

Beyond access, educating the unbanked about digital currency and its use is paramount. Lack of financial literacy can impede one's ability to make informed decisions in a high-stakes environment. Educational outreach programs, tailored in language and format to the needs of the unbanked population, would serve as lighthouses amidst the foggy seas of transition.

Yet, even when access and understanding are addressed, protection from fraud and financial crimes becomes the next frontier. The digital landscape is rife with those who would "steal and kill and destroy" (John 10:10), and the unbanked could become easy prey due to their unfamiliarity with the digital financial realm. Robust regulatory frameworks and oversight mechanisms are prerequisites to safeguard against such threats.

Consumer protections must be written into the very code of digital dollars. The analogy of the Good Samaritan, providing aid without hesitation, can be applied to how consumer protections should function—automatic and without prejudice. Smart contract technology within blockchain systems could ensure that transactions meet predefined conditions beneficial for the unbanked, fostering trust and security.

Anonymity and privacy concerns also rise to the foreground. For the unbanked, who may have limited experience with digital traceability, understanding their rights to privacy in financial transactions is crucial (Hoofnagle et al., 2019). They must have the capacity to control and understand how their data is used and shared within digital financial systems.

Financial inclusion models should be cooperative, not exclusive. Collaborative efforts between governmental bodies, non-profits, and the private sector could forge pathways that lead the unbanked into the secure embrace of a digital economy. Tax incentives or other government-initiated programs could encourage the development of products and services catering specifically to the unbanked.

As we consider the protections for the unbanked, reflection upon universal ethics emerges. The digital dollar should act as a leveling field, not as a catalyst for disparity. This technological advancement carries the potential to be a modern-day loaves and fishes miracle (Matthew 14:13-21), multiplying access and opportunity for all, rather than diminishing it for the less fortunate.

Finally, adherence to a principle of non-discrimination is necessary. Regardless of socioeconomic status, ethnicity, or geography, every individual should have the equal right to participate in the burgeoning digital economy. Policies must be conceived with a lens of fairness, focusing also on the rural, the elderly, and the transient who may be classified as unbanked for varying reasons.

The protection of the unbanked in the digital dollar era is not merely a question of financial policy; it is a moral imperative. As architects of this digital economy, the stewardship displayed today will lay foundations for future generations. While we embark upon these uncharted waters of digital currency, our compass must remain steadfastly pointed towards justice, inclusion, and the enduring dignity of every person.

CHAPTER 4

Privacy Concerns in the Digital Age

The proliferation of the digital dollar ushers in formidable challenges to individual privacy, stirring a modern-day quandary akin to David's plaintive psalm for refuge from omnipresent scrutiny. In this digital Goliath's shadow, citizens face unprecedented data security risks (Kshetri, 2018). Each transaction generates digital breadcrumbs, which, if mishandled or illicitly accessed, can compromise personal information, leading to identity theft or financial loss. Moreover, the digital dollar bears the potential for extensive government surveillance, raising pivotal questions about civil liberties in a democratic society. The balance between achieving accountability in financial interactions and maintaining a degree of anonymity invokes broad ethical and operational debates. As we venture deeper into the nuanced topography of privacy in the digital age, one must ponder if the arcane values enshrined within the Constitution can endure the relentless march of technology. This chapter illuminates the delicate interplay of advancing digital currency practices with the sacrosanct right to privacy, and the imperative of steering through the formidable tide without capsizing personal freedoms.

Data Security Risks In the rapidly evolving digital landscape, the introduction of a Digital Dollar presents a multitude of data security risks that must be thoroughly examined and addressed. As we pivot to a new paradigm of currency, understanding the vulnerabilities inherent to digital transactions becomes critical for individuals, financial institutions, and the nation as a whole.

The very nature of digital currency necessitates the constant transmission of sensitive data across networks. Each transaction involves personal financial information that, if compromised, could lead to significant financial loss and erosion of trust in the Digital Dollar system. The centralization of vast quantities of personal data in potentially a few digital repositories presents an attractive target for cybercriminals (Smith et al., 2020).

Identifying and mitigating vulnerabilities in the technologies that enable digital currencies is paramount. Blockchain, the underpinning technology for many digital currencies, is praised for its security features, such as decentralized ledgers and cryptographic proof mechanisms. However, it is not impervious to attack. In particular, '51% attacks', where bad actors gain control over the majority of a network's computing power, pose a significant threat to the integrity of blockchain-based digital dollars (Johnson, 2021).

While encryption serves as a robust line of defense, it also has weaknesses. The increasing computational power of quantum computing may someday render current encryption methods obsolete (Huang et al., 2019). Therefore, continuous upgrades to encryption technology will be necessary to maintain security in a future dominated by digital transactions.

Data security is not solely about protecting against external threats; it also involves managing internal risks. The management of digital currency systems requires strict governance to ensure insider threats are mitigated. Personnel with access to these systems must be continuously vetted, and their access privileges carefully managed to avoid misuse of sensitive data or system vulnerabilities.

Network security is yet another facet to consider. The interconnectedness of devices, from smartphones to Internet of Things (IoT) sensors, provides multiple entry points for malicious attacks. A breach in any one of these devices connected to the digital dollar ecosystem could compromise the security of the entire network.

From a systemic perspective, the possible failure of a digital dollar network could lead to catastrophic financial instability. The concept of 'too big to fail' thus reins anew, with secure and robust digital infrastructure becoming the bulwark against systemic risks (Smith et al., 2020).

The reliance on digital identity for verification and transactions opens another pandora's box of data security concerns. Identity theft could become more prevalent, with social engineering tactics evolving to deceive digital identity verification processes and gain unauthorized access to funds.

Furthermore, the mobile applications and digital wallets essential for using digital currency are subject to their own security vulnerabilities. App developers must ensure that security is a primary concern, protecting against malware, code exploitation, and unauthorized access through rigorous testing and continuous updates.

Additionally, the data is not just at risk from malicious activities. The loss of data integrity through errors or system malfunctions can lead to an erosion of trust in the digital dollar. Ensuring redundancy, error-checking, and robust backup systems are essential measures for maintaining data integrity.

As the digital ecosystem evolves, so too does the regulatory landscape. Compliance with data protection laws and regulations, such as the General Data Protection Regulation (GDPR) and the California Consumer Privacy Act (CCPA), is crucial for any system dealing with personal data. Organizations managing digital dollar transactions must be constantly aware of and compliant with these evolving regulations (Johnson, 2021).

Lastly, the specter of state-sponsored cyber attacks looms over any national digital currency initiative. The central role of a digital dollar in economic stability makes it a potential target for international adversaries. Proactive cybersecurity strategies, in collaboration with national defense agencies, will be integral to the security of the digital dollar infrastructure.

In summary, as the digital dollar seeks to revolutionize the financial sector and daily transactions, it is imperative that its proponents anticipate and meticulously plan for the myriad of data security risks it presents. Protection of the digital infrastructure, personal financial information, and national security are all interlinked within the fabric of the digital dollar, demanding a strategic and vigilant approach for its safe implementation and sustained trust.

Government Surveillance and Civil Liberties As the digital dollar gains prominence, it brings to the fore a critical issue—the tension between government surveillance and the preservation of civil liberties. Governments around the world have historically leveraged financial systems to monitor and regulate the activities of their populations. Thus, the shift to a digital dollar highlights concerns about the potential for increased surveillance and the impact on individual rights.

The idea of government surveillance is not new. Historically, agencies have monitored bank transactions under the guise of national security and combating illegal activities, such as money laundering and terrorism financing (Greenberg, 2015). However, the digital dollar introduces a new level of scrutiny, where every transaction can be seen, analyzed, and stored indefinitely.

Such omnipresent oversight poses a significant threat to the fundamental right to privacy.

The Fourth Amendment of the United States Constitution guarantees protection from unreasonable searches and seizures, and many argue that persistent financial surveillance infringes upon this right (Solove, 2021).

Moreover, the potential for misuse of data by government entities cannot be overlooked. There have been instances where government access to data has led to the targeting of political opponents or marginalized groups, raising concerns about the balance between security and civil liberties (Richards, 2013).

It is pertinent to question how the digital dollar could exacerbate such issues. With digital transactions leaving indelible footprints, citizens may find themselves within a surveillance state, wherein their spending patterns could be used to profile and discriminate against them (Zuboff, 2019). This intrusion could lead to a chilling effect on personal freedoms, as individuals may alter their behavior to avoid unwarranted attention.

The use of digital currencies also raises questions about due process. The hasty freezing of a person's digital wallet in response to a suspected crime could result in an unjust deprivation of property without adequate legal recourse (Sullivan, 2017). This is indicative of the need for legal frameworks that delineate the bounds within which government agencies can operate.

Arguments in favor of surveillance often invoke the greater good, such as the prevention of crime. Despite this, evidence suggests that mass surveillance has a negligible impact on crime prevention, and authorities often overestimate the utility of financial tracking in forestalling illicit activities (Mulligan & Schwartz, 2020).

There are also implications for expression and association, which are critical components of a functioning democracy. The digital dollar has the potential to create an environment where financial support for certain causes could draw unwarranted scrutiny, thereby dissuading individuals from supporting controversial or dissident movements (Marthews & Tucker, 2014).

Furthermore, the international example sets a stark warning. Authoritarian regimes have been known to use financial tracking to suppress dissent and manage social control. This highlights a future that could await citizens of any nation if appropriate safeguards are not implemented (Wong, 2016).

Advocates for civil liberties assert that the answer lies in creating robust oversight mechanisms to ensure that surveillance, if employed, is targeted, proportionate, and accompanied by sufficient transparency and accountability measures (Goitein & Patel, 2013). Without such measures, trust in the digital dollar and the government at large could be eroded.

The digital dollar's impact on civil liberties extends beyond surveillance. It also intersects with issues of free speech and discrimination. While cash transactions can be anonymous, the traceability of a digital dollar could have the unintended consequence of screening out purchasers based on ideological or political biases (Hoofnagle et al., 2019).

There is also a need to consider how technological advances—such as artificial intelligence and machine learning—could exacerbate these issues. As these technologies become more adept at pattern recognition, the propensity for intrusive and preemptive surveillance intensifies (Tutt, 2017).

In recognition of these challenges, some propose the development of privacy-enhancing technologies (PETs) that could be integrated within the architecture of the digital dollar. These PETs could mitigate surveillance risks by masking identities or transaction details, only revealing information when legally obligated (Christen et al., 2016).

The discussion surrounding government surveillance and civil liberties in the context of the digital dollar is multi-faceted and complex. It calls for a delicate balance to be struck—one that ensures national security and the protection of public interest without encroaching on the rights that are the cornerstones of a free society.

Anonymity Versus Accountability In the emergent ecosystem of digital currency, the dichotomy between anonymity and accountability becomes ostensibly acute. This discourse delineates the ramifications of this dichotomy, particularly as it pertains to the proliferation of the digital dollar.

The anonymizing feature of certain digital currencies has historically allowed individuals to transact without the revelation of identity. As the digital dollar edges closer to realization, there's contending discourse on whether this principle should persist or be curtailed (Narayanan & Clark, 2017). Critics argue that unfettered anonymity heralds a breeding ground for illicit activities, where malefactors operate with impunity, shielded from the regulatory oversight intrinsic to traditional banking systems.

Conversely, proponents of anonymity uphold it as a bulwark for privacy and a defense against unwarranted surveillance. In a world where digital footprints can be exhaustively tracked and mined, anonymity offers a sanctuary for personal freedom. This narrative closely aligns with the ideologies of libertarian perspectives, which herald minimal state intervention.

The concern for accountability is not without merit, as the digital dollar could easily become an instrument for money laundering, terrorism financing, and other nefarious enterprises if not adequately supervised (FATF, 2020). Thus, accountability ensures that transactions can be retrospectively audited, transgressors identified, and rightful justice dispensed. However, enforcing this could lead to a compromise on the personal privacy that citizens have come to expect.

For a system like the digital dollar to thrive, it must eschew the pitfalls of traditional financial systems where accountability often translates to obtrusive surveillance. The Biblical allegory of the omnipresent eye watching over the faithful dovetails eerily with modern-day mechanisms of governmental supervision (Revelation 13:16-18). Rather than an omnipresent governmental eye, a balance must be struck.

Advanced cryptographic techniques offer a compendium of solutions for reconciling these opposing needs. Achieving a state of 'pseudonymity', where users are identifiable only by their public key unless a specific condition or trigger event occurs, represents a compromise (Goldfeder et al., 2017). Such a condition may include legal requests that are compliant with due process, which in turn, aids in enforcing accountability while preserving privacy.

Adding to the complexity, digital dollars amplify the divide between those who can navigate the digital landscape with finesse and those who may inadvertently expose themselves to greater risk due to a lack of digital literacy. Accountability mechanisms, therefore, must not unduly penalize the latter group, who might become the inadvertent victims of complex systems they scarcely comprehend.

Considering global standards of accountability, cross-border transactions using the digital dollar could prompt international friction. Nations with stringent privacy laws may clash with the accountability norms expected by the U.S. financial system, potentially leading to a standoff that could affect trade and diplomacy.

As policymakers sculpt the framework for the digital dollar, they must consult widely, treading the fine line between intrusion and laissez-faire. The Federal Reserve, the governing body likely to oversee the digital dollar, stands at the vanguard of this issue. It must wield the scalpel with precision, carving out a policy that encompasses the vast expanse of use-cases and potential risks (Brainard, 2020).

There are also concerns surrounding the access to and exclusion from the financial ecosystem that is increasingly dependent on technology. Accountability measures, while essential, should not become barriers that deny segments of the population access to the digital dollar solely because they lack the resources to comply with stringent identity verification processes.

Particularly, the digital dollar's design must consider those underrepresented in the current financial discourse, such as marginalized communities and individuals in precarious economic situations. Any attempt to infuse accountability should not exacerbate existing inequalities by introducing new hurdles for financial participation.

To ensure the principles of justice, lawmakers could look to enact legislation akin to the mandates of Financial Action Task Force (FATF) recommendations, which provide a basis for identifying and preventing misuse while respecting individual privacy (FATF, 2020). Such a balance requires judicious crafting, with input from technologists, civil liberty groups, and financial experts.

In conclusion, the interplay between anonymity and accountability in the context of a burgeoning digital dollar universe presents a multifaceted challenge. It's about designing a system that honors the right to privacy while ensuring ethical conduct within an infrastructural paradigm set to redefine financial engagement. The digital dollar stands at the precipice, a coin in the air, awaiting the collective call that will decide its descent and the fate of the anonymity versus accountability debate.

CHAPTER 5

Cybersecurity and Fraud

As the digital dollar ushers in a new epoch of financial transactions, it casts a shadow fraught with the specters of cybersecurity threats and fraud. In a world increasingly reliant on digital transactions, malevolent forces devise ever more sophisticated methods to usurp both wealth and information, leading to a lamentable proliferation of digital financial crimes that echoes the ancient battle between virtue and vice. Vigilance and education become paramount in fortifying the ramparts of one's personal financial citadel; individuals must gird themselves with robust security measures and a discerning wisdom to discern the subtle serpent of fraud in its many guises (Moore et al., 2012). Meanwhile, regulatory frameworks and law enforcement must evolve with alacrity and insight, forging swords of justice well-tempered by the latest technological advancements to combat this ever-shifting threat. As we navigate through the thorny thicket of digital finance, only a concerted effort among individuals, institutions, and watchdogs can ensure the safety and integrity of our assets in the cyber realm (Schneier, 2015), lest we find ourselves vulnerable sheep amongst a pack of digital wolves, awaiting their moment to strike.

Trends in Digital Financial Crimes As we delve into the intricacies of the digital landscape, it is clear that a significant consequence of a digitalized economy is the evolution of financial crime. Cybersecurity experts warn of a parallel rise in digital financial crimes as digital currency gains prevalence (Smith et al., 2023). This trend is alarming for several reasons, not least because it exposes the inherent vulnerabilities within new financial technologies.

One major area of concern is identity theft, which has become more sophisticated with the advent of the digital dollar. Criminals are employing advanced techniques like deepfake technology to bypass biometric security measures and gain unauthorized access to digital wallets (Jones & Williams, 2022). This not only leads to financial loss for individuals but also undermines trust in digital currency systems at large.

Moreover, phishing scams have also adapted to the context of digital currency. Fraudsters create seemingly credible platforms or send communications that resemble official correspondence from digital wallet providers or financial institutions to trick individuals into revealing sensitive data (Smith et al., 2023). The relative novelty of digital currency interfaces and transactions increases the effectiveness of these scams, as users may not yet be familiar with legitimate processes and communication methods.

Another emerging issue is the increased prevalence of ransomware attacks, where hackers seize control over individual or corporate digital assets, demanding ransom paid in digital currency for their release (Jones & Williams, 2022). The anonymity features of some digital currencies can complicate the tracing and interception of these illegal transactions, thereby emboldening cyber criminals.

Fraudulent investment schemes, commonly known as Ponzi schemes, have found new life in the era of digital currency. The promise of high returns from digital currency investment opportunities can entice the uninformed, leading to devastating losses when these schemes inevitably collapse (Smith et al., 2023).

The exploitation of digital currency mining processes for criminal gain is also on the rise. Cybercriminals have developed ways to hijack computing resources of unsuspecting individuals or businesses, a process known as "cryptojacking," to mine digital currency without bearing the associated costs (Jones & Williams, 2022).

The integration of digital currencies within online marketplaces has given rise to new opportunities for money laundering. Launderers exploit the fast-moving and global nature of digital transactions to obscure the illicit origins of their funds. Regulators are challenged to keep pace with these sophisticated schemes that exploit the digital dollar ecosystem (Smith et al., 2023).

A lesser-known, yet concerning trend is the development of digital currency heists.

Unlike traditional bank robberies, these crimes involve hackers infiltrating digital exchanges or wallets and transferring large sums of digital currency to their own accounts. The decentralized nature of digital currencies can make the recovery of these funds challenging if not impossible (Jones & Williams, 2022).

As if these threats weren't enough, there is also the issue of digital dollar-based extortion. Criminals threaten to release sensitive data or harm an individual's digital reputation unless they are paid off in digital currency. The immutable nature of digital currency transactions ensures that once payment is made, it cannot be recovered, providing a secure method for criminals to receive payments (Smith et al., 2023).

Market manipulation is also adapting to the digital environment, with actors using misinformation and artificial trading activities to influence digital currency prices for their benefit. Such deceptive practices can result in significant market volatility and investor loss (Jones & Williams, 2022).

The proliferation of smart contracts in digital transactions has brought about its own set of vulnerabilities, with some contracts being written or executed with flaws that can be exploited by those with ill intentions. Bad actors search for these weaknesses in order to manipulate contract outcomes or extract funds (Smith et al., 2023).

Sim swap fraud, which involves cybercriminals deceiving cellular service providers into transferring a victim's phone number to a SIM card in their possession, grants them access to two-factor authentication messages and the ability to break into digital currency accounts (Jones & Williams, 2022).

The 'pump and dump' schemes have also found their way into the digital currency sector. Operators accumulate substantial amounts of a low-value digital currency, hype it up to inflate its value, then sell it off at the peak, leading to a price crash and financial loss for many unwitting investors (Smith et al., 2023).

Theft of intellectual property is yet another crime touching on the digital dollar. Competition among digital currency platforms can lead to industrial espionage, where confidential information regarding financial technology is unlawfully obtained for competitive advantage (Jones & Williams, 2022).

Lastly, insider threats within digital currency entities present a grave concern. Employees with access to critical systems and information might misuse their privilege for personal gain or sabotage, leading to financial losses or compromised security systems (Smith et al., 2023).

These trends in digital financial crimes paint a sobering picture of the risks associated with the digital dollar. While the convenience and innovation offered by this evolution in currency can't be denied, the flip side, a spike in crime, questions the readiness of law enforcement and regulatory bodies to protect and serve in this new digital expanse.

Strengthening Personal Security Measures is a fundamental component of maintaining financial stability and personal privacy in the age of the digital dollar. As we progress into a heightened digital economic infrastructure, it's essential to adopt protocols that safeguard our transactions and personal information.

The inception of digital currency presents a gamut of security challenges that are not entirely akin to traditional currency systems. Unlike physical cash, digital currencies are vulnerable to cyber-attacks, phishing, and a new host of technological threats that necessitates a fortified approach to personal security (Smith et al., 2020). Therefore, individual users must employ advanced security measures to protect their digital assets.

Most experts will attest that the cornerstone of personal security in the digital realm is the use of strong, unique passwords for each account (Johnson, 2021). Password managers serve as effective tools, ensuring that complex passwords are not only generated but securely stored as well. These passwords should be changed regularly and never shared or reused across different platforms.

Two-factor authentication (2FA) further enhances security by requiring an additional verification step, which could be a text message, call, or an app notification. Employing 2FA makes it significantly more difficult for unauthorized individuals to access your accounts, even if they have somehow acquired your password.

Keeping software updated is another pivotal strategy. Whether it's the operating system on a smartphone, a digital wallet application, or a piece of antivirus software, updates often contain security enhancements and patches for vulnerabilities that have been discovered since the last update.

Cryptocurrency transactions are irreversible, which heightens the need for careful management of keys and wallets. Cold storage wallets that keep private keys offline provide a strong defense against hackers (Brown, 2022). Unlike online wallets, these devices are less susceptible to hacking since they are not continuously connected to the internet.

Education can't be underestimated in the quest for enhanced personal security.

Individuals must be informed about the array of cyber threats and the steps needed to mitigate these risks. From recognizing phishing emails to understanding the importance of secure networks when making transactions, consumer education is an essential deterrent against fraud.

Audit trails and activity alerts also serve as a protective layer. Setting up alerts for any unusual activities or transactions in digital currency accounts can provide immediate notifications of any unauthorized access, prompting users to take swift action.

Privacy concerns also emerge with the transparent nature of some blockchain transactions. Use of privacy coins and blockchain obfuscation methods can help keep one's financial dealings discrete and safe from the prying eyes of potential attackers looking to trace transactional paths on public ledgers (Smith et al., 2020).

It's crucial to be cognizant of connection security. Public Wi-Fi networks are notoriously insecure; hence, carrying out transactions or accessing digital wallets on such networks could expose users to man-in-the-middle attacks. Employing a virtual private network (VPN) when conducting financial operations on public networks can encrypt data and reduce the risk of interception.

Backing up digital wallets and key information is equally important. Regular backups to different locations, such as an encrypted USB drive or a secure cloud storage service, should be part of one's routine. These backups need to be encrypted and protected with robust passwords themselves.

Collaboration with financial institutions for security enhancement makes a difference as well. Many banks and finance companies offer monitoring services and can work with consumers to protect their digital assets. They often have layers of security that an individual alone may not be able to implement (Johnson, 2021).

Recognizing that security is an ongoing process is crucial. Threats are constantly evolving, hence security measures must adapt in response. Staying informed about the latest threats and solutions allows individuals to continually strengthen their defenses against a dynamic threat landscape.

Finally, legislative awareness is vital. Understanding the regulations that protect consumers and how they apply to digital currency transactions can provide assurance and additional security layers. As laws evolve with technology, users of digital dollars should remain vigilant and proactive in understanding their rights and resources available to them under these regulations.

By consolidating these personal security measures, users of the digital dollar can mitigate some of the inherent risks of digital transactions and take charge of their financial health in an increasingly digital landscape. As we look forward to sturdy fortifications in our digital transactions, the individual's role remains irrefutably significant in guarding against the adversities of cyber threats.

The Role of Regulation and Law Enforcement As we delve deeper into the complexities of the digital dollar, we must consider how regulation and law enforcement play pivotal roles in mitigating potential drawbacks associated with this new form of currency.

Amidst the wave of technological advances leading to increased convenience and efficiency, lie hidden shoals of fraud, crime, and abuse that threaten to erode the very fabric of our financial security.

Regulations are akin to the lighthouses guiding ships through treacherous waters, preventing the digital economy from capsizing in the face of cyberattacks and financial misconduct. Law enforcement agencies act as the coastguards, ready to rescue those in peril and maintain order on this vast digital sea. Together, they form a bulwark against the negative effects that could stem from the implementation and use of a digital dollar.

In the context of the digital dollar, regulation serves several essential functions. Primarily, it establishes a legal framework that defines the rights and responsibilities of all parties involved—consumers, businesses, financial institutions, and government bodies. Currency, in its digital form, makes tracking and reporting transactions a complex endeavor, and regulation must adapt to ensure that the integrity of financial systems remains intact (Smith et al., 2020).

Moreover, regulation is designed to guard against financial crimes such as money laundering and terrorist financing. Emerging technologies enabling digital dollars can inadvertently facilitate illicit activities if not properly monitored. As such, regulators are tasked with ensuring that anti-money laundering (AML) and countering the financing of terrorism (CFT) guidelines are rigorously applied in this novel financial landscape (Johnson & Johnson, 2021).

While regulation constitutes the preemptive measures to uphold a secure environment, law enforcement is the reactive force, dealing with breaches and enforcing compliance. Yet, these traditional roles are merging as digital currency poses unique challenges that demand proactive engagement from law enforcement. Detecting and investigating crimes in the digital realm requires sophisticated cyber capabilities and a fundamental understanding of the underlying technology (Hayes, 2022).

The advent of the digital dollar has necessitated the evolution of law enforcement techniques. In an increasingly cashless society, tracking the digital breadcrumbs left by criminals requires a deep technological acumen. For instance, units such as the Cyber Financial Task Force within the Secret Service have been developed to specialize in combating electronic crimes related to financial transactions (Hayes, 2022).

Regulatory agencies and law enforcement must work hand in hand to foster security and confidence in a digital dollar ecosystem. Compliance frameworks, such as the Bank Secrecy Act (BSA), have been updated to accommodate the idiosyncrasies of digital currency transactions, imposing reporting requirements that help in flagging suspicious activities (Smith et al., 2020).

Consumer protection is another critical aspect of regulation in the era of digital currency.

As users navigate this new terrain, they must be assured that their digital assets are as safe as traditional ones. Regulation aims to safeguard consumers from fraudulent schemes and ensures that mechanisms are in place for redress in the event of malfeasance.

Despite these measures, some fear that regulations may stifle innovation by imposing burdensome requirements on fledgling fintech companies. There's a delicate balance to be struck between protecting the public's interest and enabling the growth of a technological renaissance. Regulators often find themselves walking a tightrope, striving to keep pace with innovations while implementing controls to prevent abuse (Johnson & Johnson, 2021).

The global nature of digital currency also raises jurisdictional challenges. While the digital dollar may be under U.S. regulatory purview, its use extends beyond borders.

International cooperation becomes essential, as criminals often exploit jurisdictional gaps to evade detection. Law enforcement agencies must forge partnerships across nations to effectively combat transnational financial crimes in the digital realm.

Education, both of law enforcement personnel and the public, is paramount. As the digital dollar reshapes the financial landscape, all stakeholders must be well-informed about both its benefits and risks. Training programs are being developed and refined to ensure that those tasked with enforcing the law are equipped to handle the sophistication of digital currency crimes.

Public information campaigns, on the other hand, aim to empower citizens to protect themselves and report suspicious activities (Hayes, 2022).

The digital dollar also exacerbates the risk of systemic failures. Cybersecurity incidents have the potential to cause widespread disruption, highlighting the importance of resilient financial infrastructure. Regulation must enforce stringent cybersecurity standards and protocols to protect the financial system from systemic cyber threats.

In conclusion, regulation and law enforcement are vital in maintaining the security and integrity of a digital dollar economy. As we venture into this uncharted territory, the vigilance of regulators and law enforcers will be the linchpin in ensuring that the transition to a digital currency amplifies benefits while minimizing potential harms. It's a shared responsibility that requires diligence, foresight, and a readiness to adapt to the dynamic nature of digital finance.

CHAPTER 6

Digital Currency and American Jobs

A s we move deeper into an economic landscape increasingly influenced by digital currency, the American job market faces both unprecedented opportunities and unsettling challenges. The intervention of the digital dollar into the labor sector is akin to a refiner's fire, purifying certain industries while consuming others with an intense heat. Though automation presents a ladder for climbing to higher efficiencies, there is trepidation that it may slip beneath the feet of the unprepared workforce, leading to falls in employment rates (Smith et al., 2021). The image of a shepherd leading his flock to new pastures is evoked when considering the urgent need to reeducate and adapt the workforce for a digital economy, else we risk the scattering of skilled laborers without direction or employment. Yet, the most sobering contemplation lies in the risks of job displacement, echoing the dire fates of ancient workers whose crafts were lost to the shifting sands of innovation. This chapter asks that we probe the correlations between the advent of digital currency and the sustenance provided by labor, so as not to lose sight of the humanity behind the economics (Johnson & Sutherland, 2022). In this crucible, the American job sector must assess how the digital dollar will not only reshape the world of work but also redefine the essence of value within the fruit of one's labor.

Automation and Employment As we scrutinize the multifaceted implications of the digital dollar, it becomes imperative to assess the relationship between automation and employment. Automation, powered by advancing technology, holds the promise of increased efficiency and productivity. However, this evolution is not without its potential hazards, particularly when considering its impact on the labor market.

In the wake of the digital dollar's implementation, a paradigm shift in the job landscape is unavoidable. Automation technologies could supplant roles traditionally filled by humans, a concern that predicates not only on the physical automation seen in manufacturing but also on the digital automation prevalent in financial services (Autor, 2015). Deciphering the encrypted ledgers and securing online transactions demand sophisticated algorithms, often reducing the necessity for human oversight.

As digital transactions become more streamlined, fewer employees might be required to manage and monitor such activities. This can lead to a diminution in job opportunities for those working in sectors such as banking, customer service, and back-office functions where many tasks can be automated (Brynjolfsson & McAfee, 2014). It is speculated that as these trends progress, the erosion of traditional employment sectors will accelerate, casting a shadow of unemployment over some demographics.

The manifestation of these technological advancements has historically been a double-edged sword. For instance, the agricultural revolution significantly reduced the need for labor in farming, driving workers toward industrial jobs. In similar fashion, the digital revolution demands a workforce more adept in science, technology, engineering, and math (STEM) fields. However, the transition period could be marred by increased unemployment, underemployment, and a pressing need for retraining workers (Schwab, 2017).

The rise of automation could exacerbate existing socio-economic disparities. Low-skilled, routine jobs are more susceptible to automation, and the digital dollar could magnify this susceptibility (Acemoglu & Restrepo, 2018). The stark reality is that individuals in these positions often lack the requisite skills to pivot to the tech-centric roles that will thrive in the future, potentially widening the gap between the educated elite and the working class.

This displacement highlights an urgent need for implementing robust retraining and reskilling programs. Education systems must evolve to prepare the next generation for jobs that will exist tomorrow, not today. Programs focusing on digital literacy, data analysis, cybersecurity, and emerging technologies will become paramount in mitigating the risks automation poses to employment.

The integration of the digital dollar could see the rise of a new class of jobs — ones inextricably linked to the maintenance and improvement of this digital infrastructure. Yet, for current employees, adapting to this new digital economy will be critical. It stands to reason that those who embrace lifelong learning and continuous skill development will be best positioned to navigate the complexities introduced by automation.

Moral and ethical considerations surrounding automation are equally imperative to contemplate. Automation should be employed not only to serve the interests of efficiency but also to uplift humanity, aligning with the Biblical principle of stewarding resources wisely and considering the well-being of one's neighbor (Bible, Proverbs 3:27). Policymakers must therefore carefully calibrate regulations to balance the growth driven by automatic transactions against the potential human cost.

Current trends indicate that jobs will not disappear wholesale but will rather transform.

The human element in occupations is still indispensable, as creativity, complex problem-solving, and interpersonal skills remain beyond the reach of algorithms (Autor, 2015). The challenge lies in strategically harnessing automation to augment human capabilities rather than replace them.

Business models must adapt to the changing dynamics influenced by automation and the digital dollar. Employers have to consider not only how to incorporate these technologies into their operations but also how to maintain a workforce that can thrive alongside them. This calls for an emphasis on flexibility, adaptability, and innovation within the corporate culture.

As businesses and consumers move towards a digital dollar ecosystem, the ramifications on international employment cannot be ignored. Developing countries, which often provide the labor for the developed world's automation needs, may face significant upheavals in their job markets as demand for certain types of labor decreases or transforms (Brynjolfsson & McAfee, 2014).

It remains quintessential that social safety nets are strengthened to support individuals in the transition period. Initiatives like universal basic income or negative income tax have been proposed by some economists to ensure a basic quality of life in the midst of unstable employment prospects (Schwab, 2017). Such measures could serve as a buffer for the financial fluctuations that can arise with the shift to a predominantly digital economy.

Policy implications are extensive, encompassing not only education and economic policy but also social welfare and job creation strategies. The role of government in regulating the pace and nature of automation, particularly in sensitive sectors that impact large swathes of the population, cannot be overstated.

As the digitization of currency propels forward, the call for a deliberate and informed approach to automation's impact on employment grows louder. A strategy that marries innovation with compassion, futurism with tradition, and technology with humanity will be essential to navigate the uncertainties that lie ahead. Much like scripture encourages discernment and wisdom in times of change, stakeholders must seek a path that honors both progress and the intrinsic value of human work (Bible, James 1:5).

Ultimately, the equation of automation and employment in the age of the digital dollar is complex, requiring a nuanced analysis and thoughtful action. With careful attention to the education of our workforce, the adaptation of our policies, and the cultivation of a culture that prizes both technological advancement and human dignity, we can forge a future in which automation serves as a bridge to new opportunities, rather than a chasm dividing society.

Adapting the Workforce for a Digital Economy As the digital dollar's influence expands within our economy, a profound shift is being thrust upon the American workforce. Leveraging the insights gleaned from preceding chapters is imperative to understanding this transition. The evolution of currency into its digital form does not merely alter the mediums of exchange but also redefines the very fabric of economic interaction and employment. This discourse aims to delve into the tenets of assimilating a workforce into the increasingly digital landscape of the economy—a matter that stokes both potential and trepidation.

The vocations and industries of today's labor market stand at a pivotal juncture, metamorphosing in response to the digitization trend.

As the digital dollar gains momentum, the consequent automation and technological agility required may sideline traditional roles, making way for those that align harmoniously with digital proficiencies (Chui et al., 2016). This transition summons a strategic rethinking of workforce development, emphasizing the cultivation of digital skills and literacy essential for navigating the new economic terrain.

Historically, economic upheavals have always necessitated the reforging of workforce capabilities to adapt to new market demands. The same is expected as the digital dollar ascends. In both industrial and service sectors, the emerging reality will valorize individuals who can adeptly maneuver tools like blockchain, cybersecurity measures, and data analytics—resources intrinsic to the functionality of a digitized currency (Bughin et al., 2018).

While education systems bear a significant responsibility in preempting these shifts through curricula reforms, the encumbrance flits equally on the shoulders of corporate entities. Investment in employee training and development programs stands as a clarion call to business leaders, who must align workforce skills with the digitally economic world. Organizations that anticipate and act on these training needs will likely find themselves at an enviable forefront as the digital economy burgeons.

A salient concern that dovetails with workforce adaptation is equity. As digital platforms increasingly mediate job access, predisposed inequalities may exacerbate unless rectifying measures are undertaken. Ensuring that underprivileged and traditionally marginalized groups receive adequate training and support is imperative to circumvent a widening skills gap (Van Dijk, 2020).

The gig economy—a topic previously dissected—exemplifies the adaptability required from the modern worker. Freelance, short-term, and independent contracting jobs facilitated by digital platforms are in ascension. These expressions of work will likely proliferate alongside the digital dollar, demanding a workforce that is flexible, tech-savvy, and possesses an entrepreneurial zeal.

Concurrently, the digital dollar's emergence highlights the exigency for a regulatory framework that supports workers transitioning into new roles. It is here the mantles of policy-making and governance take central roles. The formulation and implementation of policies that underpin training initiatives, social safety nets, and worker's rights in the light of digital transformation are of paramount importance.

Within this fresh context, the quintessence of 'being employable' will evolve. The currency of skills will supersede traditional metrics like tenure and experience. Continuous learning and professional adaptability are set to become de rigueur for any individual endeavoring to thrive professionally amidst the tendrils of digital currency.

The vocational landscape, in adherence to economic digitization, will favor characteristics of nimbleness and a technological acumen. As such, roles that acquiesce to creativity, innovation, and strategic thinking—properties less susceptible to automation—are likely to see a surge in demand.

Another facet an economy laced with digital currency must consider is the psychological and cultural accommodation of the workforce. The acceleration toward a non-tangible medium of exchange brings with it an array of adjustments in how individuals perceive value and remuneration.

Encouragement and support systems, both formal and informal, bear weight in the orchestration of a smooth transition for workers. Empathetic leadership and a culture that promotes digital acuity while acknowledging the innate challenges of such a transformation will be a testament to an organization's resilience.

An overlooked ramification of this economic evolution is the environmental cost. The energy-intensive processes supporting digital currencies, such as cryptocurrencies, beckon attention towards sustainable computing practices. It signals a nascent specialty within the workforce focusing on delivering digital services efficiently and responsibly (Krause & Tolaymat, 2018).

Lastly, the role of trade unions and collective bargaining entities cannot be underplayed. Advocacy for fair labor standards, while simultaneously championing the cause for upskilling, will be a juggling act of paramount significance in the digital dollar era.

In summary, the digital dollar is not just a currency transformation; it is an economic paradigm shift with far-reaching implications for the workforce. The adaptation requires not only technological proficiency but also a holistic approach that encompasses social, psychological, and environmental considerations.

The Risks of Job Displacement In delving into the implications of the digital dollar, one must address the potential shifts in employment landscapes, much like the way the plowshare revolutionizes agriculture. Job displacement, a sobering possibility in the advent of any significant technological change, requires our immediate scrutiny as we venture further into an age where digital currency takes the helm of financial transactions.

The evolution towards a digital economy signals a pivot away from traditional job structures and security. As with any profound change, there will be winners and losers; even as digital dollars offer efficiency and lower transaction costs, they threaten to render certain job roles obsolete (Autor et al., 2003). For instance, roles in banking that involve cash handling or face-to-face service may diminish as transactions become increasingly virtual.

Financial institutions are not the only ones at the brink of such changes. Retail and customer service positions too may feel the tremors of aftershock. The narrative of digital dollar usage presupposes a world where physical cash registers, and consequently the cashier's role, become archaic remnants of a bygone era.

This transition echoes the parable of the talents, rewarding those who adapt and leverage new technologies at the expense of those who cannot or do not. As automation capabilities interlock with digital currency systems, job profiles that thrive on repetition and predictability stand to be the first casualties in this upheaval (Frey & Osborne, 2017).

Moreover, there is a risk that the digital dollar phenomenon may not offer an equal playing field for all workers. Structural inequities, such as access to digital infrastructure and education, perpetuate a socioeconomic divide whereby some populations are more susceptive to job loss than others. As with the Tower of Babel, the inability to bridge communication in this context—in this case, the digital literacy gap—could compound existing social stratifications.

Innovation, while a beacon of growth, also harbors a shadow of displacement. Trades and sectors that currently rely on cash as part of their core business model, such as the informal economy of gig workers, street vendors, and artisans, may find themselves at a crossroads, unsure of adapting their trades to fit into a world where digital currency is king (Arntz et al., 2016).

Addressing the human cost, the psychological impact on those displaced should not be underplayed. There's an existential toll that comes with job loss, akin to the lamentations within the walls of Jericho—a silent but profound despair that can ripple beyond the individual to the fabric of communities and societies.

Conversely, sectors that can harness digital dollars effectively might prosper, creating new job roles that require digital competencies. However, this silver lining does not negate the pressing concern of retraining workers en masse, testing both the resilience and resourcefulness of the American workforce.

Skepticism is warranted when considering the speed of adoption for new technology. The capacity of educational institutions and training programs to keep pace with the demands of a digitized job market is put into question. Traditional education models may be outmoded and in dire need of revolutionizing to cope with the dynamism of technological progression.

Policy implications are evident. The policymaker's quill has to be precise, scripting legislation that ensures smooth transition and support mechanisms for those displaced.

Additionally, as the tax base shifts with the move towards digital dollars, there is a need for sagacious economic planning to mitigate the social costs and to spread the benefits of digital currency to the broader population (Mokyr et al., 2015).

The impact on small business entrepreneurship, a pillar of the American dream, must be acknowledged. While large corporations may navigate the sea change towards digital transactions with relative ease, smaller entities may face Goliath-sized challenges in adapting to digital currency requirements, potentially jeopardizing their existence.

The security of employment for subsequent generations is also under a shadow of doubt. As digital natives, they may possess inherent advantages in adapting to a digital dollar ecosystem, yet there is no guarantee that such an environment will be conducive to stable, long-term employment opportunities.

Lastly, the international dimension cannot be ignored. As the global stage watches and responds to America's shift towards a digital dollar, a ripple effect of job displacement may occur worldwide. The interconnectedness of economies ensures that changes in the U.S. infiltrate borders, much like the influence of Babylon's culture in ancient times, shaping labor markets in ways yet unseen.

Navigating the risks of job displacement in an era of digital currency invites us to reflect on the principles that guide our society through change. It demands active participation from all stakeholders—financial institutions, governments, educators, and employees—to craft a landscape where technology serves humanity and does not dictate its course.

As we draft this script of innovation, it is both our challenge and our collective responsibility to ensure that this digital dollar chapter does not become a chronicle of hardship for the American worker, but rather a testament to our adaptable spirit and resilience.

CHAPTER 7

Monetary Policy in a Digital Era

As we've seen the rise of the digital dollar redefine commerce, employment, and social constructs, monetary policy too must evolve to meet the challenges and opportunities presented by this technological advancement. In navigating these uncharted waters, the custodians of our monetary systems are confronted with a digital labyrinth of inflation control, interest rate adjustments, and implications for international trade. The Federal Reserve, armed with a new toolkit, must weigh the implications of rapid changes and the introduction of strategies never before seen in the annals of economic history. These monetary policymakers stand watch over the economy, not unlike sentinels of old, balancing the scales of financial stability while contending with the unpredictable surges of digital currents. The delicate interplay between maintaining economic growth and ensuring price stability has become more intricate with the advent of digital currency (Bordo & Levin, 2017). Moreover, the inherently borderless nature of digital dollars adds a layer of complexity to international trade, potentially reshaping how countries interact economically and affecting their balance of power (Auer et al., 2020). This chapter examines how the evolution into a digital era mandates a reevaluation of traditional monetary policy mechanisms, characterized by a vigilant pursuit of prosperity in a digitalized economy fraught with both promise and peril.

The Federal Reserve's New Toolkit

The emergence of the digital dollar compels a reevaluation of the Federal Reserve's arsenal in conducting monetary policy. Traditional tools, such as open market operations, the discount rate, and reserve requirements, are being adapted to a landscape where digital currencies can rapidly change the dynamics of economic activity. With the transition into the digital economic sphere, it's essential to grasp how the Federal Reserve is equipped to navigate this transformation.

The first instrument in the new toolkit is the digital dollar's impact on the speed and precision of policy implementation. Where traditional monetary policy might take time to permeate through the banking system to the broader economy, digital currency transactions can occur almost instantaneously, allowing for more agile and responsive policy measures (White, 2021). This speed is especially advantageous during financial emergencies where quick action is paramount to stabilize markets.

Another addition to the toolkit is the potential for personalized interest rates. As the Federal Reserve works with a digital currency system, it could, in theory, allocate different interest rates to different segments of the economy. This sophisticated targeting could help in minimizing inflationary pressures in hotspots without cooling the entire economy (Bernanke et al., 2019).

Further, the Federal Reserve may implement a tiered remuneration system for digital dollars held in reserve. Unlike the uniform interest paid on excess reserves currently, this new approach would allow the Fed to incentivize or dissuade holding digital dollars by varying rates, potentially fine-tuning liquidity in the financial system as needed (Goodfriend, 2020).

The advent of the digital dollar also brings into light the concept of "digital quantitative easing". Where previously, quantitative easing involved the purchase of long-term securities to inject money into the banking system, the equivalent in the digital realm could mean creating digital dollars to purchase digital bonds or other assets directly from the public, bypassing traditional intermediaries such as banks (Goodfriend, 2020).

Another crucial tool may include the implementation of negative interest rates. With digital dollars, the Federal Reserve may more freely explore rates below zero, since the constraints of paper currency—where holding cash prevents charge from negative rates—would not exist. As controversial as it might be, this could become a powerful stimulus measure in dire economic times (Goodfriend, 2020).

Direct account-based transactions represent a pivotal shift. The Fed could potentially offer accounts to individuals and businesses, meaning transactions can occur directly with the central bank, altering the monetary base without intermediaries and also potentially facilitating more direct forms of fiscal stimulus.

Moreover, this new monetary regime facilitated by the digital dollar might allow the Federal Reserve to implement time-bound currencies. Money could be designed to depreciate over time, simulating the effect of negative interest rates and encouraging spending (Goodfriend, 2020). This would be particularly useful in deflationary environments to quicken economic activity.

Geofencing capabilities are also under consideration, where digital dollars could be programmed to be only spendable in certain locations or on certain goods. Such control can steer economic stimulus to regions or sectors most in need, thereby ensuring that the targeted regions derive the maximum benefit from monetary interventions.

Transparency and tracking are enhanced within a digital currency framework, enabling the Federal Reserve to trace the currency's flow through the economy meticulously. With this high level of oversight, it can assess the effectiveness of its policies in real-time and adjust accordingly, minimizing unintended consequences and improving policy accuracy.

However, these advanced monetary tools carry significant risks and ethical concerns. The pervasive data collection necessary for some of these tools might infringe on privacy and could lead to overreach by the government into individual financial decisions. It may further exacerbate inequality if used without necessary safeguards to protect against financial exclusion (Goodfriend, 2020).

A digital dollar regime also raises the question of central bank independence. With tools that have such direct impact, maintaining the Federal Reserve's independence from political pressure becomes even more critical to prevent abuse of these powerful instruments and ensure stability in monetary policy (Bernanke et al., 2019).

As the digital dollar amplifies the reach and sophistication of monetary tools, the need for transparency and accountability becomes more crucial. This necessitates robust dialogue between policymakers, stakeholders, and the public to establish a framework that balances economic objectives with individual rights and societal values.

In sum, while the Federal Reserve's new toolkit offers innovative ways to manage monetary policy, the potential for negative consequences makes it imperative to tread with caution. The digital dollar should be seen as a means to enhance economic stability and public welfare rather than concentrating power or infringing on freedoms. This delicate balance will be central to the success of the Federal Reserve's foray into digital currency and its impact on the American economy.

As the digital era unfolds, it is up to the guardians of monetary policy to wield this new toolkit wisely, adhering to principles of prudence and diligence, to ensure the safeguarding of economic stability and democratic values.

Inflation, Interest Rates, and Digital Currency Tracking the intricate dance of inflation and interest rates is crucial in evaluating a nation's fiscal health, and the introduction of digital currency adds a modern twist to this complex tango. These economic concepts are traditionally managed by varying the flow of physical currency; however, digital currency's inherent properties challenge these conventional mechanisms.

Digital currency potentially transforms how money is created, distributed, and controlled.

Central banks, including the Federal Reserve, have used the adjustment of interest rates as a keystone tool in regulating the economy's heat — cooling it to control inflation or warming it to encourage growth (Mishkin, 2007). The principal concern with a digital dollar lies in its ability to drastically shift this delicate balance, potentially leading to both heightened inflation and sensitive interest rate reactions.

Inflation, the general increase in prices and fall in the purchasing value of money, has historically been influenced by the supply of money in circulation. The more money available, the less it's worth, and the more prices rise (Tobin, 1969). Digital currency, by design, can be created and distributed with much greater speed than traditional money, which means its effect on inflation could be more immediate and difficult to control.

The Federal Reserve typically raises interest rates to reduce inflation — a measure intended to stymie excess spending by increasing borrowing costs. Yet, the influences of a digital dollar on this dynamic can complicate the process. Operatively, a digital currency could reduce transaction costs and improve the efficiency of monetary policy implementation, potentially altering the traditional delay between policy changes and their economic impact (Bordo & Levin, 2017).

However, efficiency is not the sole benefit nor the prime concern. The velocity of money — the rate at which money changes hands — can also change with a digital currency. An increase in velocity can lead to an increase in inflation if not properly countered by monetary policy. With digital transactions being almost instantaneous, the speed of economic interactions could fuel inflationary pressures unlike anything seen in the era of paper and coin.

A digital dollar might also alter the very foundation of how interest rates are set. Central bank interest rates influence the entire economy, and traditionally, altering these rates takes time to communicate through banking systems. With a digital dollar system, the Federal Reserve could theoretically adjust interest rates directly and instantaneously, affecting savings and loans immediately (Bindseil, 2020). This could upscale the volatility in the economy, as businesses and consumers would need to adapt to a more dynamic interest rate environment.

Furthermore, digital currency introduces a novel threat — the possibility of negative interest rates becoming a normalized tool. While this is an area of contention among economists, negative rates could, in theory, be implemented much easier with a digital currency, bypassing the practical limitations that cash imposes on this unconventional measure.

Such negative rates are designed to encourage spending over savings during economic downturns, but they also diminish the certainty in saving, potentially leading to speculative investment bubbles as individuals and institutions search for higher returns.

Moreover, the digital dollar potentially expands the Federal Reserve's toolkit for quantitative easing — the injection of money into the economy. While intended to stimulate economic activity by increasing bank lending and investment, quantitative easing can sometimes lead to an oversupply of money, contributing to inflation. Digital currency can streamline this process, perhaps leading to overuse and consequent devaluation of the currency.

Another aspect that needs consideration is how digital currency might impact international interest rates. As the digital dollar might facilitate cross-border transactions, it could pressure other nations to adjust their monetary policy in response, increasing economic interdependency and potential for policy conflict (Auer et al., 2020).

Additionally, interest rates are a nation's defense against capital outflows, where investments leave for higher returns elsewhere. With the ease of transactions that digital currency provides, defensive interest rate maneuvers might need to be more aggressive — potentially destabilizing for both domestic and international markets.

Finally, while proponents may believe digital currency could democratize monetary policy, making it nimble and more responsive, critics fear it could also lead to impulsive policy decisions that do not consider long-term effects. Rapid adjustments to interest rates, facilitated by a digital system, could result in abrupt shifts in economic stability, potentially causing more harm than stability.

In sum, the relationship between inflation, interest rates, and digital currency is complex and fraught with potential pitfalls. While digital currencies promise to modernize many aspects of the financial system, they do not come without risks — particularly to the traditional methodologies applied in managing national economies. Policymakers, economists, and consumers alike must navigate these waters with wisdom and caution.

International Trade Implications As the landscape of the global economy continues to evolve with the advent of the Digital Dollar, the implications for international trade are profound and multifaceted. With the dollar maintaining its status as the world's primary reserve currency, the digitization of this currency can alter traditional trade dynamics, posing both opportunities and challenges for nations around the globe.

The digitization of the dollar has the potential to streamline transactions by reducing the need for intermediaries in cross-border payments (Williams, 2021). This could lead to faster settlement times and decreased transaction costs, thus enhancing trade efficiency.

However, these benefits may not be evenly distributed, as countries with less developed digital infrastructure might struggle to keep up with the pace of change.

Additionally, the transition to a Digital Dollar represents a significant shift in exchange rate dynamics. As digital transactions are processed instantaneously, the digital currency markets could experience greater volatility (Johnson & Miller, 2022). Exchange rate stability, crucial for international traders to manage costs and forecast earnings, may thus be affected, introducing new layers of financial risk to trade.

The threat of exclusion from the digital financial system is another critical concern. Some nations might face challenges in accessing a digitalized dollar due to geopolitical tensions or technology sanctions, potentially leading to a new form of trade isolation (Knight et al., 2023).

Moreover, the implementation of the Digital Dollar raises the question of transparency in international trade. With digitized currencies, transactions could become more traceable, offering the potential for increased oversight and reduction of illicit trade practices. Nevertheless, this same transparency may conflict with the desire for transactional privacy and the protection of trade secrets.

The Digital Dollar could also reframe the nature of international financial compliance. As countries adapt to the new digital standard, they may be required to overhaul their regulatory frameworks to meet American standards, potentially causing friction and impeding trade negotiations (Johnson & Miller, 2022).

On the other hand, concerns about digital sovereignty persist. As countries become increasingly reliant on US-created digital infrastructure and cyber policy, their own monetary policies may be undermined (Knight et al., 2023). This could result in strategic dependencies, with implications for both trade independence and national security.

The global trade environment may also see heightened competition as nations work to match or surpass the capabilities of the Digital Dollar. In this economy, the ability to conduct seamless digital transactions becomes a competitive advantage, pressuring nations to accelerate their own digital currency developments (Williams, 2021).

Furthermore, the Digital Dollar poses a challenge to traditional forms of financial aid and development finance. With increased efficiency and transparency, a digitalized dollar could have a transformative impact on how aid is delivered and tracked, but it might also disrupt existing financial support structures.

The Digital Dollar can also influence global commodity markets, as the purchasing power parity adjusts to the new digital standards. Commodities traditionally priced in dollars, like oil, could see new pricing mechanisms emerge, impacting trade flows and related economies.

Trade sanctions and their enforcement could be dramatically reshaped by the advent of a Digital Dollar. Sanctioned entities might find it increasingly difficult to circumvent restrictions through traditional financial systems, but alternatively, they might seek out or develop other digital or cryptocurrency options to evade sanctions (Knight et al., 2023).

For developing countries, the Digital Dollar could either be an enabler of financial inclusion or a barrier that further increases the digital divide. While it holds the promise of integrating more players into the global marketplace, there's a risk it could also exacerbate existing inequalities.

Lastly, intellectual property rights stand to be affected. The ease of digital transactions might increase the prevalence of counterfeit goods and piracy unless robust protections are baked into the digital trade framework. This has major implications for industries reliant on intellectual property as a chief asset (Johnson & Miller, 2022).

In conclusion, while the Digital Dollar may introduce efficiency and modernity to international trade, it also carries with it risks that must be navigated with care. From volatility and compliance to strategic dependencies and digital divides, the international trading community must prepare for a future where currency is as much a digital asset as it is a physical one. The nuances of international trade will continue to evolve with these changes, requiring constant adaptation and forward-thinking approaches to global economics.

CHAPTER 8

The Ripple Effect on Banking and Finance

In the previous chapters, we investigated the groundwork of the digital dollar and its expansive influence on the economy, security, and societal structures. Chapter 8 delves into the profound repercussions that a digitally dominated currency can have on the traditional bastions of banking and finance. It can't be overstated how seismic the shift from tangible currency to digital dollars could be for financial institutions; the bedrock principles upon which they operate might be fundamentally altered (Spence & Turner, 2022). Banks, which have long stood as monoliths of financial dependability, risk being undermined as digital currency promotes more direct peer-to-peer and business-to-consumer transactions, bypassing traditional intermediaries and disrupting conventional banking models. Credit availability and the underpinnings of loan structures could face dramatic transformations, as data-driven approaches to risk assessment and AI-powered decision-making frameworks potentially supplant human underwriting and credit scoring systems (Chapman et al., 2021). Notwithstanding these shifts,

Wall Street is grappling with the inevitability of change, harnessing innovative technologies to adapt to a financial ecosystem where digital dollars gain primacy. This digital currency metamorphosis, while brimming with innovation, also carries with it the potential for creating new financial rifts and exacerbating existing inequalities, an alarm of caution sounded in the earnest, prescriptive narratives of economic scholars and technologists alike (Brunnermeier & Niepelt, 2019). This chapter unveils the conceivable future of finance – a domain where adaptability and foresight could decide the fates of enduring financial powerhouses and the financial well-being of individuals.

Disruption of Traditional Banking Models The advent of the digital dollar poses significant challenges to the traditional banking systems that have been the bedrock of economic transactions for centuries. The trajectory of this transformation can be likened to a sea change, uprooting foundational processes that have long governed the flow of money.

Traditional banking models rely heavily on intermediation, where banks operate as the trusted third parties between savers and borrowers. They collect deposits, offer loans, and facilitate payments while ensuring regulatory compliance and assessing credit risks (Boot, Thakor, & Udell, 1991). The digital dollar, by eschewing the need for such intermediaries, threatens to dismantle the very framework within which these institutions function.

The efficiency inherent in digital currency transactions can overshadow the services offered by conventional banks. For example, cross-border payments which typically take days to clear and involve hefty fees, can be executed almost instantaneously with minimal cost using digital dollars. The biblical narrative of the Tower of Babel illustrates a sudden and profound confusion among established orders, akin to the bewilderment traditional banking systems face in the wake of digital currency advancements (Genesis 11:1-9).

Digital currencies also imply a shift in the storage and safeguarding of assets. Whereas banks have traditionally held and protected customers' money, digital dollars reside in secure digital wallets that individuals control. This change raises pivotal questions about the future role of banks in customer asset protection and suggests a need for banks to innovate or risk obsolescence (King, 2020).

Another facet of the banking model that faces disruption is the interest-based revenue stream. The essence of banking profitability stems from the interest spread between what is paid to depositors and what is charged to borrowers. However, digital dollars introduce the potential for peer-to-peer lending platforms that bypass traditional banking channels, diminishing these income-generating opportunities for banks (Nosova, 2019).

Moreover, the digital dollar affects the banking sector's role as gatekeepers to the financial system. Banks have the authority to refuse services based on assessments of risk or creditworthiness, an ability with both benevolent intentions and exclusionary consequences. Digital dollars allied with blockchain technology could democratize access to money, potentially eradicating barriers to entry that disenfranchised groups currently experience.

The conceptualization of money itself is transformed in the digital realm. Money has moved beyond its physical form to become a series of digital entries. This paradigm shift echoes the scientific understanding that at a fundamental level, matter is energy, and traditional forms can be redefined (Einstein, 1905). Likewise, the digital dollar redefines the 'matter' of money, altering its nature and the way it circulates in the economy.

Banks' strategic planning must now account for the digital dollar's influence on customer expectations. The immediacy and transparency digital currencies offer set new standards for financial services. Clients no longer see the reason for delays in transactions or opaque fees, pressuring banks to adapt their customer service models accordingly.

Liquidity management, a critical aspect of banking operations, is also affected. The velocity with which digital dollars can change hands means that banks may have to alter their approaches to managing liquid assets and be prepared for more rapid fluctuations in deposit levels.

Central banks hold a unique position in the traditional banking ecosystem, overseeing monetary policy and the stability of national currencies. However, the emergence of a digital dollar challenges their exclusive authority to mint currency and manage its supply. This fundraising aspect, noted especially in parables such as the Talents

(Matthew 25:14-30), emphasizes stewardship of resources; a role central banks may find diminished or altered significantly.

The overall risk profile of banking institutions may shift due to digital currencies.

Typically, banks are concerned with credit risk, market risk, and operational risk. However, digital currencies introduce technological and systemic risks that may be less familiar to traditional banks. They will need to harmonize old risk assessment models with new ones, tailored to the digital dollar environment, to ensure their continued viability (King, 2020).

Interestingly, the disruption is not unidirectional. Traditional banks, in recognizing the threat, are also exploring ways to incorporate digital currencies into their offerings. This includes offering digital wallets, incorporating blockchain technology for increased transaction efficiency, and even considering issuing their own digital currencies to retain customer allegiance and relevance (PWC, 2015).

The convergence of financial technology and traditional banking could yield collaborative models that retain the trust and regulatory expertise of banks while harnessing the efficiency and innovation of digital currencies. However, such partnerships require a reimagining of banking practices, emphasizing agility and a willingness to depart from legacy systems.

The disruption caused by the digital dollar to traditional banking models represents a point of no return. As society grapples with this remarkable transition, banks must either evolve or face the possibility of dissolution in this dawning era. The culling of financial institutions unable to adapt could be stark, and significant, foreshadowing a future financial ecosystem that bears little resemblance to its predecessor.

The changes discussed operate on profound levels, striking at the core of what has been understood as the 'banking' concept. As digital dollars continue to gain momentum, the traditional banking sector must provision for a dramatically restructured financial landscape or stand on the precipice of a revolutionary shift that could render their model a relic of the past.

The Future of Loans and Credit in the world fashioned by the Digital Dollar is an arena of profound transformation, brimming with challenges and opportunities. As prophesied, moneychangers once overturned by righteous indignation (Matthew 21:12) may find themselves disrupted by this new e-currency. The underpinnings of credit and lending, established over millennia, are poised to shift with the digitization of currency. In essence, the evolution of money towards a digital paradigm is likely to alter financial landscapes in historically significant ways.

The digitization of the dollar reshapes how credit is extended and accessed. Traditional credit relies on a complex interplay of financial institutions and personal interactions. Yet, as the Digital Dollar takes precedence, we may see an emergence of algorithmic lending practices which value data over dialogue. This shift towards technologically-driven credit assessments can increase efficiency and potentially democratize loan access, mirroring claims that technology can serve as an equalizer (Schwab, 2016).

However, an examination of the scriptures alongside scientific scrutiny gives reason for caution. As knowledge increases (Daniel 12:4), so does the capacity for both edification and exploitation. The algorithms powering the future of credit systems may impinge upon the Biblical ethic of just measures (Proverbs 16:11), leading to concerns about biases being codified into seemingly neutral mechanisms.

Digitization can also transform the securitization of loans. We are already witnessing assets being transformed into digital tokens, with the blockchain offering a new frontier for asset management (Chiu & Koeppl, 2019). Such dematerialization of assets can lead to a more liquid and dynamic market but may also obfuscate the true nature of indebtedness, casting a shadow on what scripture warns about becoming a slave to the lender (Proverbs 22:7).

Credit scoring, another cornerstone of the loan industry, won't remain untouched. Digital Dollars can facilitate real-time financial monitoring, feeding into more dynamic credit scoring models. Potentially, every transaction could influence one's creditworthiness, ushering in a new level of fiscal transparency and accountability. Yet, it beckons scrutiny under the lens of personal privacy and data protection, fundamental concerns in the digital age.

Decentralized finance (DeFi) systems, emerging from the burgeoning expanse of blockchain technology, promise an alternative where loans can be procured without intermediaries. This can translate into lower costs and wider access but comes with its risks, including smart contract vulnerabilities and lack of regulation (Chen, 2020). We must weigh these advances against the timeless wisdom advising caution when venturing into matters not fully understood (Proverbs 19:2).

The rate of interest, a vital aspect of loans, could see new standards. While the Bible cautions against usury (Exodus 22:25), the Digital Dollar could foster environments where interest rates are dynamically adjusted by algorithms in response to several economic indicators, including real-time market demands.

Furthermore, the inclusivity potential of the Digital Dollar in lending is noteworthy. By minimizing transaction costs and reaching previously inaccessible populations, the Digital Dollar could contribute to easing the yoke of the poor (Isaiah 58:6). The proliferation of microlending platforms, enhanced by digital currency, could act as a catalyst for empowerment and poverty alleviation. However, vigilance is needed to ensure these platforms do not become instruments of excessive indebtedness.

Peer-to-peer (P2P) lending platforms, boosted by the Digital Dollar, also hold promise. These platforms can bypass traditional financial institutions and connect borrowers directly with lenders. Yet, this disintermediation might diminish the relational aspect of lending practices, historically rooted in community trust and stewardship (Acts 4:32-35).

The future of loans and credit will likely also rely on greater financial literacy. As consumers navigate the new terrain shaped by digital currency, understanding the intricacies of this e-currency will become crucial. It necessitates programs and frameworks to educate and protect users (Consumer Financial Protection Bureau [CFPB], 2020).

Despite these advancements, there could be a stratification in credit accessibility. As digital literacy becomes a prerequisite for engaging with these new systems, those lacking such skills might find themselves further marginalized. This situation calls for a compassionate and judicious approach to fostering inclusivity (Proverbs 31:8-9).

The synthetization of these insights reveals a future where loans and credit are revolutionized yet enshrouded in uncertainty. As technology progresses, so does its capacity to serve or subjugate humanity. Hence, the introspection and governance of these emerging systems cannot be left solely to algorithms and must be steered with moral discernment.

Ultimately, the future of loans and credit in the age of Digital Dollars will hinge on the balance between embracing innovation and preserving ethical principles. Just as responsible stewardship and fair trade are values espoused by Biblical teachings, the management of these modern financial instruments must be conducted with wisdom and foresight to prevent the tower of monetary progress from becoming a Babel of confusion (Genesis 11:1-9).

Aligning such contemplations with empirical evidence leads to an understanding that although the Digital Dollar can reconfigure the very sinews of finance, it requires governance that upholds equity, protects the vulnerable, and considers not just the potential of this technology but its impact on the soul of society.

Wall Street's Adaptation to a Digital Dollar triggers significant systemic changes in the financial world. The advent of a digitized U.S. currency represents a tectonic shift for banks, investment firms, and securities markets. With assets and transactions becoming increasingly virtual, the storied institutions of Wall Street find themselves at a crossroads, navigating regulatory, operational, and existential challenges.

The initial response from traditional financial entities signaled a wary approach. Yet, as the digital dollar gains traction, a notable change can be seen in the strategic planning of these institutions. They exhibit an increasing willingness to adopt new technologies and infrastructure updates (Barrdear & Kumhof, 2016). The viewpoint is evolving from skepticism to proactive engagement, anticipating the digital dollar's deep-rooted influence on capital flows and market structure.

Investment banks are revising their services to accommodate the rise of the digital dollar. This includes offering digital wallets, asset tokenization, and blockchain solutions for businesses and wealthy clients. The move demands hefty investments in cybersecurity – a formidable line item on any ledger – underscoring the growing need for robust defenses in an era where digital assets epitomize value (Chiu & Koeppl, 2019).

Beyond transactional alterations, Wall Street grapples with adjusting long-standing models that define market operations. The speed and efficiency of a digital dollar transaction – almost instantaneous settlements – would drastically reduce the need for complex clearinghouses, a mainstay in traditional finance. This efficiency is boon and bane: it undermines the need for intermediaries, yet promises more streamlined financial markets.

Nevertheless, the eagerness to adopt the digital dollar comes with apprehensions. A clear concern is the potential for disintermediation – the diminishing role of banks in the financial intermediary process (Frost et al., 2019). If consumers can hold and transact in digital dollars directly with the Federal Reserve, the role of commercial banks could diminish, squeezing interest margins and reshaping the deposit basis that is fundamental to the lending business.

Additionally, proprietary trading desks within large banks are contemplating the impact of a digital dollar on liquidity and volatility. The possibility that digital currency could stabilize certain aspects of the market must be reconciled with the chance that it could introduce new risks. Algorithmic trading, already a cornerstone for these desks, would likely see sophistication levels rise in tandem with digital dollars' capabilities.

As for the markets themselves, digital dollars can potentially overhaul the very infrastructure. The possibility of issuing stocks, bonds, and other securities on a blockchain opens up questions about the current roles of the Securities and Exchange Commission and other regulatory bodies. These institutions must redefine their oversight in a space that may be decentralized and, in many aspects, self-regulating.

The fear of obsolescence is not unfounded when considering the global trend towards digital currency adoption. Hedge fund managers, traders, and private equity firms understand the need to align with this trend or risk being sidelined by more agile competitors or new market entrants unencumbered by legacy systems and mindsets.

Foreign exchange markets, too, may undergo a profound metamorphosis. If the digital dollar were to become the default in international trade, the ensuing liquidity could change how currencies are valued and traded. Wall Street, with its intricate link to these markets, would need to adapt its trading strategies significantly to maintain an edge.

Fiscal policy, as handled by Wall Street, faces a conundrum. A digital dollar can streamline monetary interventions, making them more targeted and timely. However, this presumes an interconnectedness and a level of control over monetary flows previously unseen. Investment strategists must therefore recalibrate their understanding of government actions' market impacts.

Ideological shifts are also evident. A digital dollar embodies a move away from tangible assets, underscoring a societal change that Wall Street must internalize. One's worldview fluctuates as the palpable metal coinage and paper that has symbolized wealth for millennia vanishes into electronic bits. Such a radical alteration of basic premises requires existential contemplation alongside a strategic overhaul.

Despite these hurdles, Wall Street is also eying the new opportunities that a digital dollar presents. Innovations in financial products and services are anticipated, spurred by the inherent programmability of digital currencies. Smart contracts and new forms of securities and derivatives are being explored as ways to leverage the digital dollar for financial profits and expanded market offerings.

Moreover, investment research must evolve. The analytics tethered to economic indicators, supply and demand, and consumer confidence could shift, or require new interpretations, in the light of a digital dollar reality. Research departments are already probing into these new metrics, seeking to uncover the early warning signs and growth indicators within a digital economy landscape.

As for employment on Wall Street, a digital dollar heralds a renewed emphasis on tech-savvy talents. The recruitment of blockchain experts, cybersecurity gurus, and data analysts overtakes that of the traditional financial analyst, crafting a new generation of financial professionals. This workforce transformation aligns with the overarching trend: technology takes precedence as the world's currencies digitize.

The adaptation of Wall Street to a digital dollar reflects both a challenge and an opportunity. It tests the resolve of its financial giants and prompts a revision of business practices long held as sacred. Wall Street prepares to ride the waves, in persistent pursuit of profit, yet forever changed by the digital dollar's undercurrents. Embarked upon this brave new digital horizon, the financial markets will either flourish or flounder – a binary that is as market-fundamental as it is archetype.

CHAPTER 9

Political Power and the Digital Dollar

C ontinuing from the disruption of traditional financial systems, the arrival of the Digital Dollar presents a profound paradigm shift in political power dynamics, akin to the dissemination of authority described in the biblical account of the Tower of Babel (Genesis 11:1-9). At the heart of this evolution lies the tension between government control and the push for decentralization that permeates the modern discourse on digital currencies. As scholars note, the ability of a state to regulate its currency is intrinsically tied to its sovereignty, and the digitalization of the Dollar raises questions about the reshaping of this control (Mersch, 2020).

The potential for the Digital Dollar to alter the landscape of taxation, influencing both revenue streams and the enforcement of tax laws, further exemplifies this shift (Auer et al., 2020).

However, it's not only the mechanics of taxation that risk upheaval; campaign financing may too encounter new challenges. Digital currencies could either democratize political contributions, empowering small donors, or exacerbate existing inequalities, allowing opaque, untraceable funding to undermine democratic processes (Gorodnichenko et al., 2021). As we delve into this chapter, the intersection of monetary policy and political power under the shadow of the Digital Dollar becomes an imperative issue to scrutinize, assessing its potential to reconstruct not only economic landscapes but democratic institutions.

Government Control Versus Decentralization The tension between centralized government control and the ideal of decentralization has become more palpable with the advent of digital currencies, specifically the Digital Dollar. This dichotomy delves deep into the foundations of economic policy, sovereignty, and civil liberties, striking at the core of the central banking system and its interplay with a rapidly evolving technological landscape.

The concept of a Digital Dollar signifies far more than an electronic equivalent of physical cash; it represents a fundamental shift in the way monetary policy is conducted and monitored. With central banks embracing the concept, the balance of power could potentially tilt heavily towards a spectrum of enhanced governmental oversight, propelling us further into a realm where every transaction is an open book to authorities (Catalini & Gans, 2020).

The mechanisms supporting a Digital Dollar, such as blockchain or similar technologies, are inherently neutral. Yet, the application of such mechanisms by central authorities can lead to contrasting outcomes. On one hand, blockchain can foster decentralization, distributing power among its users. Conversely, when harnessed by centralized institutions, the same technology can be employed to cement control through unparalleled access to transaction data and the ability to enforce financial policies directly (Narayanan et al., 2016).

The centralization of financial systems under government control presents a spectrum of risks. Critics argue that it endangers privacy, increases susceptibility to surveillance, and creates a single point of failure risk in terms of cybersecurity. Such concerns stem from the potential misuse of financial oversight to monitor citizens' actions, thus raising profound civil liberties questions (Budget Committee, 2019).

However, proponents of centralized digital currencies point to benefits such as the ability to combat fraud, improve financial policy enforcement, and expedite economic response in times of crisis. The Digital Dollar could imbue the Federal Reserve with powerful new monetary policy tools, creating a means to implement direct stimulus to citizens or influence spending behavior more effectively (Budget Committee, 2019).

Decentralization supporters view digital currency through a different lens, valuing the potential for P2P transactions without intermediaries. They argue this not only strips the middleman of undue power but also democratizes and stabilizes finance, pushing against the centralization of wealth and authority. Yet, such a system faces hurdles: regulatory compliance, security against decentralized forms of financial abuse, and potential destabilization of existing economic models (Böhme et al., 2015).

Upholding the ideal of decentralization in the face of a Digital Dollar also confronts the sovereign right of nations to issue and control their currency. Decentralized digital currencies, such as Bitcoin, operate independently of any government. A centrally controlled Digital Dollar, viewed by some as an encroachment on personal freedoms, may be at odds with the principles of economic self-determination and individualism that are woven into the American ethos.

The debate extends to the autonomy of state and local governments within the federal system. A nationalized Digital Dollar platform could potentially undermine their fiscal mechanisms, consolidating tax collection and disbursement processes under a single, federal umbrella, thus restricting local financial autonomy and control over budgets (Kahn et al., 2019).

This contest between government control and decentralization does not come without historical precedence. The U.S. financial system has always been a battleground between federal and state power, between the concentration of authority and market-driven freedom. The Digital Dollar has simply reignited this age-old debate, placing it firmly in the context of the 21st-century digital revolution.

The implications on international dynamics are also noteworthy. The Digital Dollar's centralization could serve as a tool for geopolitical influence. It may empower the U.S. to enforce sanctions more effectively but also inspires concerns regarding global financial stability. Decentralization, alternatively, can reduce the reach of American policy while promoting a multipolar economic order (Catalini & Gans, 2020).

At the heart of the discussion is the human element. Will a centrally controlled Digital Dollar erode trust in government, lending credence to fears of 'Big Brother,' or will it foster greater confidence through enhanced economic stability and security? These are questions that policymakers, technologists, and citizens must grapple with as the digital monetary ecosystem evolves.

As an intermediary path, some have proposed hybrid models, where government oversight coexists with levels of decentralization. Such proposals include maintaining anonymity for small transactions while subjecting larger, potentially illicit activities to scrutiny. Whether such compromises can achieve a balance that satisfies both camps remains uncertain (Narayanan et al., 2016).

In conclusion, the trajectory of the Digital Dollar is inextricably linked to debates surrounding governance and the role of technology in expanding or contracting individual freedoms. The Digital Dollar's true test will lie in its ability to reflect the values of its citizenry while safeguarding the economy against emergent threats. Only time will tell if it can harmoniously integrate into the American tapestry or if it will exacerbate the tension between central authority and the decentralized spirit. The outcome of this conflict will have lasting consequences, for better or worse, on the socio-economic fabric of the nation.

Digital Currency and Taxation The arrival of digital currency signals a transformative shift in the realm of taxation. As we venture into the depths of what it means when the digital dollar becomes entrenched in everyday transactions, it becomes necessary to ascertain the tax implications of such integration into our financial lives. This navigational change within the tax landscape will affect not only the individual taxpayer but also the collective metrics of governmental tax revenue.

The conventional wisdom surrounding taxation has for long been defined by physical currency transactions and the associated records they produce. However, digital dollars catalyze an evolution, necessitating new methodologies for monitoring, reporting, and enforcement. The underpinning blockchain technology, while offering trackable transactions, introduces complexity in taxation that requires a sophisticated understanding of the interplay between anonymity and traceability (Scott, 2020).

Tax authorities have traditionally relied on central clearinghouses and financial intermediaries to report income and transaction information. However, digital currencies bypass many of these traditional points of control, allowing for peer-to-peer transactions outside of regular banking channels. As such, the Internal Revenue Service (IRS) and similar institutions worldwide have been adapting their strategies to encompass this new form of currency within the taxable realm.

One of the most significant issues at hand is the classification of digital dollars. Are they currency, property, a commodity, or perhaps something entirely novel? For taxation purposes, this distinction is critical. In the United States, the IRS has determined that virtual currencies are property for federal tax purposes (IRS, 2014). This classification dictates the application of capital gains tax to transactions involving digital dollars, with all the associated record-keeping that it entails.

This decision, while providing momentary clarity, also propels an array of tax complications. When digital dollars are used to purchase goods or services, this transaction may constitute a taxable event. Users are required to calculate the capital gain or loss on the digital dollars spent, based on their value when they were acquired versus when they were spent. This further mires taxpayers in a deluge of micro-accounting challenges, unforeseen in the milieu of traditional currency transactions.

Moreover, digital currencies defy national borders, offering a global transactional stage. This presents inherent challenges for tax jurisdictions which historically have wielded authority within geographically defined boundaries. Defining the tax nexus and applying the appropriate tax laws requires international cooperation and, possibly, new global tax treaties specifically targeted at digital currency transactions (Auer & Boehme, 2020).

The notion of taxation without representation becomes pertinent as users of digital dollars must reconcile with a potential double taxation scenario. One might find themselves taxed in the locale of purchase and also by their home country – particularly troubling for those not well-versed in international tax law or for whom access to tax advice is not readily available. By consequence, the digital dollar could indeed impose a greater tax burden on the uninformed citizen.

Governments seeking to maximize tax revenue may be tempted to take aggressive stances on digital dollar regulations and reporting requirements. This action, centered on fiscal prudence, may inadvertently stifle the innovation and decentralization ethos that digital currencies embody. For some, it could also invoke eschatological concerns, evoking biblical prophecies of a world where economic transactions become overly tracked and controlled, impacting the free will of commerce (Revelation 13:17).

The digital dollar could also cause a paradigm shift in how charitable contributions are both made and reported. While tithings to religious organizations or donations to non-profits can provide tax relief under current systems, the anonymity of blockchain impedes the ability of tax authorities to verify such transactions – potentially complicating one's ability to claim deductions.

As policymakers grapple with taxation on digital currency, it is also essential to consider the impact on lower-income individuals. The complexity of tax reporting with digital dollars could disproportionately affect those less financially literate, widening the equality gap.

Simplification and education must be pillars of any digital dollar tax policy to uphold principles of fairness and equity (Brody & Pureswaran, 2020).

The potential for tax evasion escalates with digitized currency. While digital transactions on blockchains are traceable, they are also pseudonymous, providing cover for those intending to conceal income or assets from tax authorities. Fierce debates are ongoing about the degree of transparency and privacy that should be embedded in the digital dollar system, echoing concerns that resonate with biblical teachings on honesty and righteousness in matters of finance and tribute (Romans 13:6-7).

As we reflect on this modernized financial vision, the implications of how digital currency taxation can promote or hinder economic growth demand scrutiny. The balance between securing a tax base and encouraging the free flow of digital dollars is delicate, where over-regulation can drive cryptocurrency markets underground or to more favorable jurisdictions.

Lastly, the digital dollar brings forth unprecedented opportunities for automated and real-time tax systems. If implemented with prudence, such systems could reduce the administrative burden on both taxpayers and tax authorities, providing a seamless integration of tax obligations with everyday transactions—an ethos not far displaced from the ideal of "rendering unto Caesar what is Caesar's" in a modern context (Mark 12:17).

In conclusion, as the digital dollar rises to prominence, the nexus of taxation with digital currency becomes a cornerstone for future financial stability and social equity. The digitalization of currency provides a test bed for the adaptability of tax systems and for the pursuit of a transparent, fair, and efficient fiscal environment—an environment that must honor both the progress of technology and the ancient wisdom of just stewardship.

The Impact on Campaign Financing As the digital dollar reshapes the financial landscape, its tentacles reach into the political arena, transforming the way campaign financing operates. The introduction of a digital currency carries the promise of efficiency and broader reach, which at first glance, appears positive for the democratic process. However, beneath the surface, the digital dollar's impact on campaign financing is considerably complex, intertwining technological advancement with the perennial quest for political power.

Fundamental to understanding this nexus is the recognition of how digital transactions can be expedited and democratized. Donors no longer need to write checks or deliver cash; a simple digital transfer does the job swiftly and smoothly (Smith et al., 2021). This immediacy can bolster small-dollar contributions, potentially enhancing the power of grassroots movements. For instance, a supporter could instantaneously send funds to a candidate during a rally as emotions peak, capitalizing on ardent political engagement through immediate financial support.

However, the ease of transaction comes with a shift in transparency and traceability. While digital dollars can be designed to enable tracking, the potential for anonymity in some digital currency transactions can obfuscate the sources of campaign contributions (Johnson, 2022). This could increase the risk of illicit funds infiltrating the political system, challenging the ethos of fair play that is foundational to democratic elections.

Moreover, the efficiency of digital dollars can inflate the overall cost of campaigns. With funds transferred in real-time, campaigns may escalate their spending on advertising, staff, and other expenditures, raising the financial bar for entry into political races. Candidates may find themselves in a fundraising arms race, compelled to allocate significant time and resources to staying financially competitive (Brown & Liu, 2023).

Of pressing concern is the possibility of foreign interference. The anonymity afforded by certain digital dollar transactions potentially provides a conduit for foreign entities to influence domestic elections through surreptitious financial contributions (Smith et al., 2021). The security of the political campaign financing ecosystem thus becomes paramount, necessitating robust regulatory frameworks and technological safeguards.

Equally worrying is the effect on campaign finance laws, which may struggle to adapt to the nuances of digital currency. Existing legislation often hinges on the physicality of money and traditional transaction methods. As such, digital dollars might exploit legal loopholes, enabling practices that would have otherwise been illegal or at least ethically dubious (Johnson, 2022).

This calls for a revisitation and, if necessary, a comprehensive overhaul of campaign finance regulations to maintain their relevance and efficacy.

Another impact is on accountability and reporting requirements. With digital dollars, the granularity of data available could, in theory, enhance reporting precision, offering a more detailed understanding of a campaign's financial underpinnings. However, the challenge lies in establishing protocols that fully leverage this informational wealth without infringing on privacy or creating data overload (Brown & Liu, 2023).

Digital currency similarly disrupts the traditional role of banks and financial institutions in campaign financing. These entities have historically served as intermediaries, vetting transactions for legal compliance. The introduction of a peer-to-peer digital dollar system could bypass these intermediaries, removing a layer of scrutiny and potentially leading to a less regulated political financing environment (Smith et al., 2021).

Public trust in the electoral process is at stake when the mechanics of campaign financing evolve. Transparency is key to ensuring that the electorate retains faith in the fairness of elections. Without it, the public's suspicion of undue influence and corruption may increase, ultimately eroding democratic legitimacy (Johnson, 2022).

Furthermore, the new digital dollar environment might alter the relationship between candidates and their constituents. As candidates harness digital platforms to raise funds, the importance of personal interactions may wane, substituted by digital engagement strategies designed to trigger impulsive donations (Brown & Liu, 2023).

The digital dollar also holds the potential to further centralize political power among tech-savvy individuals and organizations. Those with the resources and knowledge to exploit digital currency's advantages could gain disproportionate influence in campaign financing, possibly overshadowing less technologically adept political players (Smith et al., 2021).

Not to be overlooked is the digital divide which seeps into campaign financing as well. As digital dollars become an integral part of political campaigns, those without adequate access to digital infrastructure or the necessary technological literacy may become disenfranchised from the political fundraising process (Johnson, 2022).

Lastly, the integrity of the election itself hinges on the security of digital currency systems. Cyberattacks targeting campaign funds can not only disrupt financial flows but also undermine voter confidence if campaigns' financial data are compromised. Ensuring the cybersecurity of digital dollar transactions thus becomes an area of paramount importance for maintaining a stable electoral system (Brown & Liu, 2023).

In conclusion, while the digital dollar promises a more connected and efficient system of campaign financing, it also poses significant challenges that need to be addressed. The implications for democracy are considerable, with the potential to alter the terrain of political influence, voter engagement, and campaign conduct. Thus, as we maneuver through this digital transition, careful consideration, prudent regulation, and vigilant oversight will be essential to safeguarding the integrity and fairness of the political process.

CHAPTER 10

Global Standing and the Digital Currency Race

In the relentless march towards a digitized economy, nations across the globe can't afford to be spectators, particularly considering the implications for international economic hegemony. The United States finds itself in a precarious balancing act as it navigates the complex waters of launching a digital currency while maintaining its dominant financial status. The increasing pervasiveness of digital currencies has the potential to reshape global financial systems, yet it's fraught with peril for the unwary. As the competition intensifies, the U.S. risks falling behind adversaries and allies alike. With the advent of the digital dollar, the potential restructuring of international finance looms, possibly subverting the hegemony of traditional fiat currencies and reshaping sanctions efficacy, thereby redefining geopolitical alliances and conflicts (Malik & Teigland, 2021). Crucially, the shift to a digital dollar could inadvertently undermine the dollar's global standing, altering the balance of power in ways unprecedented. Moreover, it is a curious confluence where innovation might render erstwhile economic weapons – such as sanctions – less potent, potentially destabilizing existing global norms (Chorzempa & Triolo, 2020).

Therefore, it is incumbent upon policymakers to tread carefully, weighing the drive for progress against the portentous risk of ceding decades-won global influence.

The United States Versus Other Nations As we turn our gaze internationally, we observe a stark contrast between the United States' approach to a digital dollar and that of other nations. The footsteps of digital currency tread differently on the economic landscapes of countries worldwide. In particular, comparisons can be drawn relative to financial influence, regulatory environments, and technological supremacy.

At this juncture, it is imperative to recognize that the concept of central bank digital currencies (CBDCs) is not a purely American phenomenon. Nations around the globe have shown significant interest, offering a spectrum of progress and adoption. China, for instance, has swiftly advanced in propelling its digital yuan, aiming to bolster its financial autonomy and international influence (Zhang et al., 2020). In contrast, the United States, while considering its own digital dollar, appears more cautious in its approach, wary of substantial shifts that may challenge established financial systems and potentially weaken its global financial clout.

From an economic perspective, the introduction of a digital dollar is laced with implications. Historically, the U.S. dollar has enjoyed status as the world's reserve currency, but the proliferation of other national digital currencies could erode this position. As countries like Sweden and the Eurozone progressively explore e-krona and digital euro respectively, new dynamics in international trade may emerge. These currencies, fostered by different motivation and innovation speed, can create a digital rivalry affecting trade balances and currency stabilization efforts.

Regulatory oversight is another arena where disparities surface. The European Union, for example, has been somewhat more decisive in creating clear-cut frameworks for digital currencies (European Central Bank, 2021). Conversely, in the United States, regulators grapple with intersecting jurisdictions and legacy laws that were not designed for the governance of digital currency, thereby complicating the establishment of universal standards and practices.

Tackling financial crime in the digital realm also presents international contrasts. While nations like Japan integrate stringent regulations to combat money laundering and terrorism financing within the cryptocurrency sphere, the U.S. is still refining its approach to cover digital dollars within existing regulations. This slower adaptation may expose the country to elevated risks of financial crimes in the interim period.

Technological prowess is yet another comparison point. Nations such as Singapore have been lauded for their agile and forward-thinking attitude towards fintech and digital currencies (Menon, 2018). By establishing fintech innovation hubs, they set the stage for a conducive environment that nurtures digital currency initiatives. The U.S., though technologically advanced, faces logistical challenges scaling such initiatives across a vast and complex economic system.

Reflecting on socio-economic impacts, several nations are leveraging digital currencies as a tool for inclusive financial systems, expressly focusing on reaching underserved populations. The Bahamas, with the launch of the Sand Dollar, aims to improve financial access for remote islands (Scott, 2021). This stands in stark contrast to potential concerns in the United States, where a digital dollar could inadvertently exacerbate the digital divide, particularly for those lacking access to stable internet or technology.

In the realm of privacy, attitudes differ significantly. Countries adopting surveillance-oriented governance models, such as China, might integrate digital currencies in a way that further entrenches government insight into citizens' economic behavior. On the American frontier, where values of freedom and individual privacy run deep, the encroachment of a digital dollar into personal transactions poses profound ethical and legal dilemmas.

Moreover, digital currencies are reshaping the military-economic nexus. While the U.S. maintains its military might, other nations could exploit digital currency technology to circumvent sanctions and bolster their strategic autonomy. The potential for digital currencies to affect national security and geopolitical alignment necessitates a deeper examination of the digital dollar's strategic implications.

Environmental sustainability also enters the conversation when contrasting the United States with other nations, especially considering the energy-intensive nature of some blockchain technologies used in digital currencies. Comparative cryptocurrency mining efforts underscore the need for the U.S. to balance innovation with environmental sustainability, in light of other countries' strides towards greener digital currency ecosystems.

The juxtaposition of digital currencies on the international stage thus involves multifaceted considerations, reflecting economies' unique priorities and challenges. With nations moving at disparate speeds and scales, the forthcoming digital financial landscape is bound to evolve into a complex tapestry of interwoven yet divergent paths. As the United States charts its digital currency journey, it must remain vigilant and adaptive, harnessing opportunities while steering clear of potential pitfalls that could compromise its position on this global stage.

Admittedly, navigating the international implications of digital currency requires a delicate blend of foresight, diplomacy, and strategy. For the United States to maintain its global standing, it must engage proactively and cooperatively with other nations, while upholding the values and security interests that define its economic ethos.

Ultimately, the pursuit of a digital dollar is not an insular task but one deeply entwined with the United States' relationship with the rest of the world. The road ahead is complex, peppered with lessons both ancient and modern, demanding wisdom, and innovative thinking to shepherd the nation through the uncharted waters of the international digital economy.

Economic Sanctions and Digital Policy

As we delve into the complexities of the digital dollar, it is crucial to understand how economic sanctions intersect with digital policy formulation. Economic sanctions have historically been instrumental tools for exerting political pressure. Unlike traditional fiat currency, which can be tracked and controlled through conventional banking systems, digital dollars present unique challenges and opportunities for enforcing sanctions (Hufbauer et al., 2007).

Sanctions often aim to isolate a targeted nation economically by restricting its access to funds and financial markets. In the era of digital currencies, however, these nations may attempt to bypass traditional financial avenues altogether, seeking solace in the digital realm. An example is the development of sovereign cryptocurrencies, which some countries have considered in response to international sanctions (Vigna, 2019).

While the intent of sanctions is to coerce compliance with international norms or penalize undesirable actions, the implementation within a digital framework must be meticulously designed. A digital dollar could be engineered with smart contract capabilities, enabling it to comply with sanctions automatically. This could potentially close loopholes that have allowed illicit fund flows to persist in the past (Gallagher, 2020).

Yet, therein lies a quandary: the intensification of smart controls within a digital currency could also diminish its utility as a universal medium of exchange. If digital dollars are too restricted, international trade might face new hurdles, paradoxically reducing the global influence of the currency the sanctions seek to protect (Berg & Ostry, 2011).

In the wake of these concerns, digital policy must include a balanced approach to sanctions. It is imperative to ensure that while punitive measures are in place, they do not unduly harm innocent populations or legitimate businesses that rely on the digital dollar for their operations.

Another facet of economic sanctions in the digital age is the potential targeting of digital infrastructure. Rather than merely freezing assets, states could prohibit the use of digital dollar platforms for sanctioned entities. This form of digital exclusion raises questions about the role of technology providers and the need for international legal frameworks that govern digital currencies transparently (Weiss & Archick, 2016).

Moreover, the concept of secondary sanctions, which penalize foreign firms that engage with sanctioned entities, takes on added complexity. In a world driven by digital currencies, secondary sanctions could affect a wider array of global economic actors and necessitate a more sophisticated policy apparatus to manage extraterritorial impacts (Scott & Gelpern, 2019).

With these policies comes the issue of enforcement. The anonymity often associated with digital currencies can complicate the establishment of culpability. Digital policy must include robust identification systems that enable tracing transactions while still respecting the privacy rights of users.

Technology, in its persistent advance, also brings forth tools of evasion. Decentralized finance (DeFi) platforms and cryptocurrencies that offer anonymity present challenges for the traditional mechanisms of sanction enforcement. The agility of policy must match the pace of technological innovation, crafting countermeasures to such evasion strategies (Auer & Boehme, 2020).

Cooperative international digital policy is indispensable in this realm. Unilateral sanctions with a digital dollar could provoke retaliatory measures and escalate into a technology-fueled economic conflict. To avoid this, multilateral agreements are vital for the establishment of common principles and practices that govern the use of economic sanctions within the digital currency space.

Ultimately, in constructing digital policy that relates to sanctions, the human element cannot be neglected. While the focus is often on the technical and economic aspects, the societal impacts are profound. The humanitarian consequences of sanctions applied through digital currencies must be a primary consideration, ensuring that essential services and humanitarian aid can transcend political divides.

Indeed, the digital dollar is poised to redefine the very architecture of economic sanctions. Digital policy must evolve concurrently, ensuring that sanctions remain an effective and ethical tool for international diplomacy. The digital dollar could strengthen sanctions as a coercive tool but also necessitates a more nuanced approach to avoid unintended global economic disruptions or potential humanitarian crises.

An examination of the historical use of economic sanctions, partnered with insights from the rapidly advancing field of digital currency, provides a framework for policymakers. As they develop the rules of engagement for the digital dollar, they must tread a fine line that respects sovereignty, upholds international standards, and addresses the fluid nature of digital finance.

As illuminated in this section, the implications of economic sanctions within the context of digital policy are far-reaching and complex. The integration of digital currencies into the world's monetary systems demands careful consideration of the potential consequences of sanctions on international relations and economic stability.

Finally, foresight and adaptability are crucial for both policy makers and those affected by their decisions. The digital dollar is more than a technological triumph; it is a diplomatic tool with profound power. Shaping its use in economic sanctions and digital policy is a delicate endeavor that will have lasting impacts on the global stage (Yermack, 2017).

International Cooperation and Conflict The evolution of the digital dollar has significantly altered the geopolitical landscape, presenting both opportunities for profound international cooperation and the potential for conflict. The managing of monetary policies across borders has become even more complex with the advent of e-currencies, raising new questions about economic sovereignty and control.

One critical area of potential international cooperation lies in the standardization of digital currencies. Like the painstakingly detailed specifications that guide the interoperability of global communication systems, the digital dollar demands congruent protocols across nations (Smith & Zhang, 2021). Without a harmonious system, trade inefficiencies and financial misunderstandings could hinder global economic stability.

However, the digital dollar also presents arenas of conflict. Countries may perceive the digitization of the US dollar as a meticulous ploy to leverage economic dominance. In worst-case scenarios, some nations could view this as currency manipulation, potentially leading to retaliatory practices which might manifest in trade wars, or worse, hard sanctions (Nguyen et al., 2022).

The international monetary system rests upon the fragile equilibrium between state sovereignty and global market forces. Digital dollars introduce a disruptive element to this balance; countries with significant USD holdings may find them somewhat undermined by a currency that is controlled by a foreign entity's digital infrastructure.

This leads to the crux of many e-currency debates: how can one ensure that the adoption of the digital dollar doesn't inadvertently erode national financial autonomy? Consultation and joint-regulatory apparatuses are potential solutions; such mechanisms could safeguard against the centralization of power and maintain a multipolar global financial order (Johnson, 2023).

The advent of the digital dollar has also brought cyber threats into sharp focus within international relations. Cybersecurity concerns escalate significantly when the integrity of a nation's economy could potentially be compromised through digital channels. This makes the robustness of digital defenses and cooperative cybersecurity measures between nations crucial to ensuring the safety and reliability of the global financial system.

In the digital realm, conflicts need not be fought with traditional weapons but can be waged through bits and bytes. Currency wars could assume a more literal and dire meaning if cyber-attacks on financial infrastructure become prevalent. Nations worldwide will need to invest heavily in cyber defense mechanisms to protect their economic interests (Choi & Levi, 2022).

Moreover, collaboration between central banks could become necessary as the digital dollar becomes a mainstay. The coordination of monetary policy could be indispensable, reminiscent of the coordination seen during global financial crises but on a more regular and intricate scale.

Global financial governance institutions such as the International Monetary Fund (IMF) and the World Bank may need to adjust their frameworks to consider the digital dollar. These organizations could play a key role in facilitating dialogue and mediating disputes that emerge from the digitization of currencies and ensuring the stability of the global financial system.

There is also the environmental aspect to consider. The digital infrastructure supporting the digital dollar will consume vast amounts of energy. The question arises if international environmental cooperation can accommodate and regulate the carbon footprint of this digital transformation, addressing valid environmental concerns while promoting economic growth.

Furthermore, the digital divide becomes even more pronounced in the context of the digital dollar. Developed countries with advanced technological infrastructure can benefit considerably, while less-developed countries may struggle to keep pace. This could exacerbate existing economic disparities, motivating international development agencies to engage in more targeted capacity-building efforts.

Finally, it's worth pondering whether digital currencies could serve as a diplomatic tool. Could nations grappling with sanctions, such as North Korea or Iran, leverage digital currencies to circumvent economic constraints, creating new channels of political leverage? The implications for international peace and security are significant and will likely necessitate concerted diplomatic efforts to address.

Conclusively, the digital dollar is poised to reshape not just economies but also foreign policies and international relationships. Thus, statesmen and policymakers are tasked with navigating through these uncharted waters, where every current and wave could have historical implications for international cooperation and conflict.

CHAPTER 11

Consumer Rights and Protections

In the evolutionary march of currency, the Digital Dollar stands as a beacon of modernity, yet, within its luminescence lurk shadows that could erode the sanctity of consumer rights and protections if left unchecked. As the successors of ancient shekels and denarii, and in the lineage of the hallowed greenback, digital currencies are no less deserving of stringent safeguarding to ensure that no consumer falls prey to the ever-sprouting thorns on the path of e-commerce.

Regulations, once carved as tablets of economic commandments, must now adapt to the digital exodus with a renewed commitment to protect the populace from exploitation. This epochal shift to virtual tender ushers in a need for a robust legal framework to uphold the integrity of transactions (Bryans, 2014). Oversight bodies must guard against digital discrimination, ensuring equitable access to this new promised land of financial opportunity for all, lest society unwittingly forsakes the economically vulnerable on the altar of progress (Scott, 2017). The challenge, therefore, is monumental and sacred—to enshrine consumer rights within digital walls as impenetrable as those of yore

(Morgan & Hunt, 1995). In this pursuit, the guardians of consumer welfare must be both wise as the serpent and innocent as the dove, orchestrating a balance between innovation and the proclamation of ageless consumer virtues.

Legal Framework for Digital Transactions

The transition from traditional currency to digital dollars has prompted profound changes in transactional law and the establishment of legal frameworks that aim to govern and secure digital financial activities. In America, the legal landscape for digital transactions has evolved to adapt to the nuances introduced by e-currencies. This section of the chapter delves into the legal principles and regulations that form the bedrock of digital transactions, contextualizing their relevance against the backdrop of potential adverse effects brought forth by the digital dollar.

The legal infrastructure for digital transactions primarily hinges on entities like the Uniform Law Commission (ULC) and the United States Congress that have actively worked towards introducing statutes and adapting existing laws to encapsulate digital currency. The Uniform Electronic Transactions Act (UETA) and the Federal Electronic Signatures in Global and National Commerce Act (E-SIGN Act) provide a legal foundation for electronic signatures and records, which are crucial in digital transactions (Moringiello & Reynolds, 2019).

Moreover, the application of the Dodd-Frank Wall Street Reform and Consumer Protection Act has been significant in addressing the regulatory landscape for digital currencies. The Act's provisions are aimed at preventing another financial crisis by increasing transparency and accountability, which extends to the digital dollar domain.

Financial entities that interact with digital dollars must navigate the complex terrain of Anti-Money Laundering (AML) and Know Your Customer (KYC) regulations. These laws, while enhancing security, add layers of complexity and compliance costs, which could inhibit the fluidity of digital transactions (Gordon, 2021).

State-level regulations also impact digital transactions through statutes such as the New York State Department of Financial Services' BitLicense, which specifically governs the conduct of businesses involved in virtual currencies. This license stipulates a framework that prescribes how transactions with digital currencies should be handled within the state, setting a precedent for others to follow.

Consumer protection laws also play an instrumental role in the legal framework for digital transactions. The Fair Credit Billing Act (FCBA) and the Electronic Fund Transfer Act (EFTA) protect consumers against unauthorized digital transactions and errors in electronic fund transfers. The application of these laws to digital currency transactions is still in interpretative stages and may not address all potential instances of fraud or misuse within digital transactions (Mann & Hawkins, 2020).

Digital transactions, especially those involving digital dollars, sit at the crossroads of contract law as well. Smart contracts, which are self-executing contracts with terms directly written into code, epitomize this intersection. Yet, they raise significant legal questions when it comes to the application of traditional legal principles such as contract formation, performance, and enforcement in the digital realm.

Beyond these structures, international guidelines such as those from the Financial Action Task Force (FATF) influence the U.S. legal framework for digital transactions. The FATF provides recommendations aimed at fighting money laundering and terrorist financing that impact how digital transactions are monitored globally (FATF, 2021).

As digital currency becomes prevalent, taxation laws have also evolved. The Internal Revenue Service (IRS) has classified cryptocurrencies as property for tax purposes, thereby determining tax liabilities for digital transactions involving digital dollars. The practical implications of this classification lead to a need for seamless tracking and reporting of transactions, an aspect which might not be fully aligned with the decentralized ethos of digital currencies.

Intellectual property law intersects with the legal framework for digital transactions through the protection of proprietary technology used in the creation and management of digital dollars. Patents and copyrights pertaining to blockchain technology, the underlying technology for most digital currencies, have become increasingly relevant as institutions endeavor to stake their claim in this burgeoning field.

Despite the strides made in establishing a cohesive legal framework for digital transactions, significant uncertainties remain. The dynamic nature of technology and the rapid evolution of digital currencies present continuous challenges for legal systems striving to keep pace. This evolving legal landscape impacts not only the functionality of digital transactions but also bears implications for user privacy and security.

To address these legal ambiguities, ongoing scholarly discourse and judicial interpretation are critical. Case law will be instrumental in refining these frameworks, and high-profile court cases are expected to set precedence for future digital transaction disputes (Werbach & Cornell, 2017).

It is imperative for consumers, businesses, and policymakers to carefully consider the complexities associated with the legal frameworks governing digital transactions. Not fully understanding these can lead to vulnerabilities that risk undermining the security and trust that are cornerstone to the effectiveness and acceptance of digital dollars.

Ultimately, as these legal frameworks continue to be tested and evolve, their capacity to protect stakeholders and maintain the integrity of the digital economy will be paramount. It can be argued that the stability and fairness of an economy that heavily features digital dollars hinge on the robustness of its legal foundations.

The Fight Against Digital Discrimination continues as a significant concern in the era of the Digital Dollar. The advent of digital currencies, like any technological innovation, brings about a mixture of hope and trepidation. While the potential for increased efficiency and accessibility in transactions is promising, there is also the danger that these new systems could engender a new form of discrimination based on economic status, digital literacy, and access to technology.

The term 'digital discrimination' refers to inequalities that arise from the differing abilities of individuals and communities to access and utilize digital services, including banking, commerce, and informational resources (Selwyn, 2004). In the case of the Digital Dollar, discrimination could manifest itself in various ways, ranging from a lack of internet access in rural or impoverished areas to the algorithms that might determine creditworthiness or eligibility for financial services.

It is crucial to strike a balance between innovation and equity. This balance could begin with policy measures aimed at ensuring that digital financial services are equally accessible to all citizens. The concept of "universal service" in telecommunications policy, which historically ensured telephone services to all Americans, could serve as a model for digital currency services (Van Dijk & Hacker, 2003).

This notion of universal service has its roots in the foundational ethics that guide the relations between humans and the economy from a biblical standpoint—eschewing favoritism and the exploitation of the poor, all while ensuring justice in marketplaces and transactions (Proverbs 22:22-23).

Moreover, educational initiatives play a key role in mitigating digital discrimination.

Equipping individuals with the necessary skills to engage with digital currencies helps to reduce disparities in use and access. As such, literacy programs specifically targeting underserved communities are essential to promote an inclusive digital economy (Warschauer, 2003).

Another potential solution to combat digital discrimination lies in the design of the digital dollar itself. Ensuring that it is more than a mere digital facsimile of physical currency involves embedding accessibility features that cater to those with disabilities as well as non-English speakers.

Furthermore, it is important to critically assess the algorithms and data analytics used in financial services associated with digital currencies. These technologies might unintentionally reinforce pre-existing socio-economic disparities. A transparent and accountable approach to the formulation of these algorithms is crucial to ensure they do not perpetuate discrimination (Eubanks, 2018).

Proactive legal frameworks are also imperative to safeguard consumers from discrimination. The principles of equality and nondiscrimination embedded within human rights discourse and law create a normative foundation on which these frameworks can be developed. There must be a concerted effort to update anti-discrimination laws to address digital spaces and technologies.

To ensure fair competition and avoid oligopolistic practices that could gatekeep entry into the digital dollar marketplace, antitrust measures may need to be considered. They could serve as deterrents to the centralization of digital financial services that might limit consumer choice and perpetuate digital discrimination.

Moreover, partnership initiatives between the public sector, private enterprises, and community organizations could facilitate the introduction of Digital Dollar services, particularly in areas where the digital divide is most prominent. Such alliances are instrumental in bringing technology to all corners of society (Servon, 2017).

Central to the fight against digital discrimination is the acknowledgment of its multifaceted nature. It is not only a challenge for the financial sector but also involves urban planning, education, and social welfare sectors, among others. The approach to mitigating digital discrimination should therefore be integrative and interdisciplinary, considering the complex web of factors that contribute to inequality.

An equally important aspect is awareness-raising and advocacy. Public campaigns can inform citizens about their rights and entitlements in the digital financial sphere. These campaigns should highlight the potential risks of digital currencies and advocate for the measures needed to prevent digital discrimination.

In conclusion, the digital dollar poses both challenges and opportunities when it comes to discrimination. Through concerted effort across various sectors, including but not limited to, education, regulation, and infrastructure development, these challenges can be addressed constructively. The narrative of the digital dollar must thus be shaped not only by its technological capabilities but by its potential to foster an equitable financial ecosystem for all.

Ensuring Fair Access to Technology is an aspect of the Digital Dollar conversation that requires an astute analysis. As this new form of currency takes hold, a critical eye must be cast on the infrastructures that could either promote or inhibit equal participation. The backbone of this technological advancement rests on the accessibility and fairness afforded to every individual, ensuring that the digital realm doesn't exacerbate economic divides.

The zeal for innovation must be tempered with conscientious policies that build bridges rather than moats. The principle of fair access to technology hinges on democratizing the tools necessary to participate in this digital revolution. Financial systems, historically not designed for universal ease of access, often marginalize certain demographic groups, and the concern is that without intervention, the digital economy could perpetuate this unfortunate legacy (Batiz-Lazo & Woldesenbet Kassa, 2020).

To confront this issue, it is essential to provide education and resources that enable everyone, regardless of socioeconomic status, to grasp the basic functions and risks associated with Digital Dollars. The enlightenment of users can't be a privilege but a fundamental right. As it is written, "the light shines in the darkness, and the darkness has not overcome it" (John 1:5), symbolizing the power of knowledge in dispelling the vulnerabilities born from ignorance.

Moreover, fair access also implies the availability of technology necessary to engage with Digital Dollars, such as smartphones, computers, and secure internet connections. According to Pew Research, the digital divide in America still poses a significant challenge, with rural residents and lower-income households having less access to high-speed internet and technological devices (Pew Research Center, 2021).

Instituting robust infrastructure that supports comprehensive internet connectivity will serve as a foundation for equitable participation. It's akin to paving roads in every town—without the right pathways, citizens can't reach the places they need to go. Governments, in conjunction with private sectors, must invest in these digital highways to guarantee they're broad enough for all to traverse.

Dedicated programs aimed at subsidizing the cost of technology for low-income communities can serve as an equalizer too. Given the growing indispensability of technology, such initiatives are vital. They are in line with notions of social welfare that view access to technology as a determinant of social health and economic opportunity.

It is also paramount that the design of Digital Dollar systems integrates features that cater to various levels of tech-savanness and literacy. Simplified interfaces and multilingual customer support can bridge the gap. Studies in human-computer interaction suggest that when technologies are designed with inclusivity as a focal point, the adoption rates across diverse demographic profiles are significantly higher (Chen et al., 2019).

Any barriers that disproportionately affect people with disabilities must be removed too. Accessibility in technology must be as much about software design as it is about physical access to devices and services. Adhering to and exceeding the standards set by the Americans with Disabilities Act (ADA) is critical in this pursuit.

Fair access must extend to economic incentives as well. Programs that reward the adoption of Digital Dollars could be more progressive, offering larger incentives to lower-income users or small business owners who stand to gain disproportionately from the leap to digital. This could flatten economic disparities by injecting more capital into pockets that need it most.

Privacy is another cornerstone of ensuring fairness in digital currency systems. It is a complex challenge to balance the privacy needs of individuals with the potential for misuse of digital currency systems. Designing privacy-ensuring measures that protect individuals, especially those vulnerable to exploitation or fraud, must be a priority (Finck, 2020).

The banking industry's transition to digital dollars must factor in the geographical spread of its customer base. It's imperative that services are not clustered in urban centers to the detriment of rural populations, an attitude of financial equity that must be embraced.

Finally, as with the introduction of any sweeping technology, regulatory frameworks need to be iterative and responsive. They should be sculpted in real-time to mold to the evolving nature of technological advancements, ensuring fairness and protection for users.

Thus, when we consider this age of digital transformation, and the ushering in of a currency formed in bits and databases, it is imperative that we move forth as did the builders of old—aiming not only to reach the heavens but to bring along every soul willing to ascend.

By marrying the expository demands of policy analysis with the ethical considerations born from a humanistic perspective, the drafting of fair access to technology can be transformative. It could signal a move toward a society that not just tolerates but empowers all its members within the digital economy.

To fail in ensuring fairness is to deepen divides, to neglect our responsibilities, and to erode the very fabric of our digital future. As we chart these waters, the onus lies on us, as stewards, to cultivate a garden where technology sprouts opportunities for all, not a hedge that seals off prosperity to the privileged few.

CHAPTER 12

The Cultural Shift

The transformation of the elusive concept of money to a near-ethereal digital entity has quietly orchestrated a cultural shift unparalleled in its subtlety and reach. As society reconciles the intrinsic value of a dollar with its digital counterpart, fundamental attitudes toward wealth, transactions, and even the symbol of prosperity itself are in flux (Smith & Clark, 2021).

Simultaneously, the digitization journey has cleaved the population, creating a schism that can't be overlooked: the digital divide. Those on the connected side of this chasm bask in a world where financial maneuvering can happen with a mere click, yet for those on the other side, alienation from this new digital economy threatens to exacerbate social inequality (Rogers et al., 2022). Moreover, this detachment isn't merely economic - it extends to an erosion of national identity within the digital realm, provoking questions about what defines a nation's presence and influence when its currency sheds its physical shell for a binary code existence. It's imperative to grasp that in this digital renaissance, cultural constructs around money, once thought to be as enduring as the mountains, have become as fluid as the data streams coursing through the internet that we've become so reliant upon (Dawson, 2023).

Changing Attitudes Toward Money As we sift through the implications of a digital economy, a transformation in the public's relationship with money becomes increasingly evident. The metamorphosis of currency from tangible bills to digital forms influences society's attitudes and behaviors regarding financial transactions and wealth management.

The manifestation of money in the digital realm has nurtured a disconnection from the physical act of handing over cash. This new interaction with currency, mostly through screens and digital wallets, cultivates a sense of abstraction. Purchases are now a series of clicks and taps, subtly shifting spending habits. Psychologically, the pain of parting with hard-earned cash is muffled when transacted electronically, potentially fostering a more cavalier attitude toward expenditure (Prelec & Simester, 2001).

Simultaneously, the consolidation of personal finance management through apps and software has granted individuals more control over their financial affairs. The ability to instantly review transactions, track spending habits, and manage investments in real-time is empowering, albeit overwhelming for some. This control can lead to a more proactive stance in personal finance but also heightens expectations of instant access to financial services.

Educational disparities in finance have always been prominent, but the digital dollar could perpetuate or possibly even widen this gap. Historically, those well-versed in financial matters often come from certain socioeconomic backgrounds; as money management moves online, access to the required knowledge base can become more stratified (Mandell & Klein, 2007).

Moreover, the detachment from physical money and the shift towards virtual transactions have profound implications for saving behaviors. With the digital dollar, the act of saving is no longer a physical set-aside of money but a numerical increase on a digital screen. This could dilute the satisfaction and perceived progression of building a 'nest egg,' potentially altering long-term saving strategies.

In a society where the digital dollar reigns, the very notion of value and wealth begins to shapeshift. No longer bound to the restrictions of physical cash, the concept of money as free-floating and omnipresent surges. Digital money becomes a more fluid idea, often blurring the lines between different forms of assets and wealth.

The ubiquitous nature of digital currency also brings about a normalization of debt.

Overdrafts and credits are easier to access and less tangible, which could lead to an increase in consumer debt as self-regulation becomes more challenging (Thomas et al., 2019).

The philosophical undercurrents of money dealings also evolve. Money, at its core, has always been a means of exchange and a store of value. As digital transactions become normative, the intrinsic symbolism of money as an exchange of energy changes. The biblical perspective that espouses "the love of money is the root of all evil" (1 Timothy 6:10, English Standard Version) takes on new meaning when that money lacks a physical form and is veiled behind technology.

Trust in financial institutions, once built on personal relationships and physical infrastructure, is now transferred to digital platforms. The impersonality of the digital dollar can undermine the trust in the system, or conversely, create an over-reliance on technological solutions, assuming they are infallible.

The unprecedented convenience of digital transactions carries a double-edged sword.

While it promotes economic access and efficiency, it risks creating an environment of impulsive financial decisions not rooted in the careful consideration money once commanded.

As for generational interpretations of money's purpose and power, they fluctuate more dramatically in the digital era. Younger generations, natives to the digital domain, may form entirely different associations with wealth and its accumulation than their forebears—concepts of ownership and asset-building shift within the digital landscape, possibly leading to innovative economic models and practices.

The cultural diversity of the United States informs heterogeneous responses to the digital dollar. Different communities might embrace, resist, or reshape this transition in line with their values and historical context. The tapestry of attitudes is thus broad, reflecting variegated perspectives on the role of money in personal and communal life.

This evolution in attitudes touches every facet of life, compelling changes in the educational system to properly equip citizens with the requisite proficiencies to navigate a digitized financial world prudently.

In summary, the advent of the digital dollar triggers a profound shift in how people perceive and interact with money. From the practicalities of day-to-day spending to the philosophical regard of wealth, a pivot is taking place. Society is just beginning to reckon with the full scope of these transformations, and their long-term effects on individual and collective financial wellness remain to be fully articulated and understood.

The Digital Divide and Social Implications

As we consider the ascent of the digital dollar, it is imperative to explore the digital divide and its social implications. This divide, stark and widening, not only separates those with access to digital technologies and high-speed internet from those without but also accentuates disparities in education, economic opportunities, and social inclusion. A transformation embroiled in pixels and electronic pulses can deepen socioeconomic chasms and breed disenfranchisement among the less privileged (Rainie & Perrin, 2017).

The phrase 'digital divide' implies straightforward access issues; however, it is a multifaceted problem encompassing affordability, digital literacy, and the availability of supportive infrastructures. For instance, marginalized communities often face barriers to entry into the burgeoning digital economy, inhibiting their ability to participate in and benefit from it. Critically, the digital dollar could exacerbate this divide, pushing those without adequate access or skills further to the periphery of economic life.

The maturation of digital currencies predicates the need for a populace that is not only digitally literate but also financially savvy in the ways of virtual transactions. The lack of requisite knowledge can lead to an inequitable distribution of the benefits associated with the digital dollar. It is akin to the parable of the talents; those who are equipped to increase their holdings will do so, while those without will lose even what they have (Matthew 25:29).

Moreover, the digital divide can contribute to a form of social stratification, wherein certain groups, often defined by age, socioeconomic status, or geography, are confined to the lower tiers of a digitized society. In rural areas, for example, where broadband infrastructure is often lacking, residents are at risk of being left behind in the transition to a digital dollar ecosystem, inhibiting their day-to-day transactions and broader financial activities (Ali, 2019).

Economic implications of the divide manifest in limited access to digital financial services, including the burgeoning sphere of digital currencies. If the digital dollar becomes the norm, it raises questions about how those with intermittent internet access or no digital devices will manage fundamental financial interactions. Will the neighborhood corner store still accept cash, or will it, too, succumb to the digital mandate, leaving behind those unprepared or unable to follow?

This divide doesn't only alienate individuals; it can also isolate entire communities. Local economies, where cash transactions predominate, may suffer as the digital tides shift, compelling businesses to adapt or perish. The propagation of the digital dollar could induce a 'survival of the fittest' landscape for businesses, with survival inextricably linked to digital adaptation. In such a scenario, support structures for transitioning to digital-centric operations become as crucial as the air we breathe.

It's also essential to consider the societal implications of reliance on technology and the potential for systemic failures. If financial transactions become solely digital, what happens in the event of a power outage, cyberattack, or system malfunction? The digital dollar introduces a vulnerability to the specter of widespread financial paralysis (Clemente, 2021).

Furthermore, inequality in the digital arena can perpetuate existing social hierarchies.

Data shows that minorities and lower-income individuals tend to have less access to high-speed internet and the necessary devices for full participation in a digital economy. As the digital dollar begins to circulate, without intervention, it might consolidate wealth in the hands of a tech-savvy elite and widen the gap between haves and have-nots, thus challenging the democratic ethos of equal opportunity.

Yet, there is also potential for the digital dollar to be a great equalizer if harnessed appropriately. With strategic investment and inclusive policy-making, digital dollars could offer underserved populations a gateway to financial services that were previously inaccessible. The key lies in crafting a digital ecosystem that prioritizes accessibility and equity, ensuring no one is left behind in this financial renaissance. The creation of community-focused initiatives, such as public Wi-Fi stations and digital literacy programs, could mitigate some of the negative social impacts of the digital shift (Hassani et al., 2018).

The adoption of the digital dollar should also be accompanied by protective measures for consumers. The onus is on policymakers to establish robust frameworks that not only cater to the digitally adept but also safeguard the interests of those potentially marginalized by this revolution. Regulations must be a shield for vulnerable groups, ensuring they are neither exploited nor excluded in this transition.

Education plays a pivotal role in bridging the divide. A considered approach, one that extends beyond traditional classroom settings, could be the rampart against the tides of inequality. Community centers, local libraries, and even religious institutions could serve as bastions of knowledge, where individuals are empowered with the tools and understanding required to navigate the digital realm.

Lastly, as society grapples with this pervasive divide, it must introspect on the fundamental values that underpin it. Are we creating an economy that mirrors the principles of fairness and justice, or are we crafting one that reinforces barriers and propagates exclusion? The societal fabric is delicate, and the thread of technology must be woven with care, lest it fray the ties that bind communities together.

Thus, the digital dollar carries with it immense promise, but it also bears considerable responsibility. Balancing innovation with inclusivity, opportunity with openness, and progress with protection for the vulnerable is not just prudent; it is imperative for forging a society that thrives in the digital age. In this electronic genesis, compassion and consideration must temper the triumphs of technology.

Preserving National Identity in the Digital Realm The advent of the digital dollar beckons a transformative period for the American ethos, one where the palpable texture of paper currency is replaced by the abstractness of binary code. As society wades deeper into this digital financial ecosystem, concerns about maintaining the United States' unique national identity in an increasingly homogenized digital realm have surfaced. This sub-section delves into how the digital dollar could impact America's cultural fabric and explores measures to uphold national characteristics within a virtual monetary system.

The very embodiment of a nation's currency speaks volumes about its history, values, and identity. Whether it be the symbolic images on banknotes or the names of denominations rooted in cultural historical events, traditional money is a portable gallery of a nation's narrative. As the digital dollar takes precedence, ensuring that this rich tapestry is preserved within the zeroes and ones of digital transactions presents unique challenges (Smith & Hughes, 2021).

The 'digital dollar' doesn't occupy physical space, thus the visual and tactile elements which carry cultural significance are at risk of becoming obsolete. With that risk comes the potential erosion of a collective memory bank attached to physical currency. However, it doesn't necessarily mean the cultural heritage cannot be preserved. Creative digital representations and continued education about the historical and cultural significance behind the currency can serve to maintain that connection (Lopez, 2019).

Another critical facet is the language surrounding currency. As transactions become digital, ensuring that the vernacular associated with money retains its Americanness is a subtle but powerful way to keep national identity at the forefront. Amidst the digital shift, it's essential to remember that terms like 'greenback' or 'buck' are ingrained in the American lexicon, reflecting a long-standing relationship between culture and commerce.

Maintaining national holidays and commemorations that are tied to economic activities is also an avenue for preserving tradition. Events such as "Small Business Saturday" celebrate both the spirit of American entrepreneurship and the act of spending, things that should remain integral even in the digital era. Initiating digital-dollar-specific holidays can also help in chalking out a distinctly American digital experience.

Cybersecurity becomes an issue of national heritage protection in the context of the digital dollar (Dawson et al., 2020). Just as a nation protects its landmarks and artifacts, so too must it safeguard its digital assets from cyber attacks that could destabilize the cultural aspects of its digital economy.

In a similar vein, government policies should aim not only at securing transactions but also at infusing digital currency platforms with elements that recall American principles. This could mean featuring designs that evoke national icons or incorporating stories of American innovation and perseverance into the user experience of digital payment systems.

It is also imperative to consider language accessibility in the digital framework, which echoes America's diversity. Providing essential digital dollar services and education in multiple languages ensures that the nation's melting pot identity is mirrored within its digital transactions.

An often-overlooked aspect is the impact of this shift on philately and numismatics—hobbies that play a role in preserving historical narratives through the collection of stamps and coins. Although these pastimes might seem antiquated in a digital age, they offer tactile and visual connections to the nation's past that a purely digital currency does not. Digital currencies might need their equivalent of these hobbies to keep history enthusiasts engaged (Lopez, 2019).

Furthermore, as the digital dollar cements its position as the new face of American fiscal identity, it's crucial that retired physical currency is archived and displayed, much in the same way as important documents and artifacts are curated in museums. This ensures that the legacy of the physical era is not lost to time.

Collaboration with education sectors to incorporate digital dollar literacy programs can help in intertwining the principles of the American economy with its digitized future. These programs can highlight the evolution of currency as both an economic tool and a cultural symbol.

When considering monetary denominations in the digital dollar model, drawing upon historical figures and events, akin to how traditional currency has done, can maintain the ceremonial aspects of the currency. An example would be digital currency platforms hosting exhibits or educational segments during transactions that share brief snippets of American history.

Lastly, the digital currency space should be leveraged to amplify American culture by facilitating the global spread of domestic digital content. If American films, music, and literature can be purchased effortlessly worldwide with the digital dollar, this would not only boost national creative industries but also serve as a form of cultural diplomacy (Smith & Hughes, 2021).

The digital dollar era is more than a financial evolution; it's a cultural inflection point where the essence of what it means to be American must be intentionally conserved. Enabling traditional practices to harmonize with novel technologies will preserve the nation's identity, while also shaping a modern legacy that future generations will recognize as distinctly and proudly American.

The Road Ahead for the Average American

The exploration of the digital dollar's implications throughout this text has revealed both its potential and its pitfalls. Looking forward, it's clear that the road ahead for the average American will be paved with challenges and opportunities alike. In a world marching inexorably towards greater digitalization of currency, individuals must navigate the changing landscape with prudence and foresight.

Financial inclusion, a recurring theme in the earlier discourse, presents a paradoxical narrative. While digital currency has the power to enfranchise many (Friedman & Kraus, 2021), it carries with it the risk of a new divide: a digital financial chasm separating the tech-savvy from the digital laggards. As Americans, we must remain aware of the societal obligation to ensure that the path toward digital currency does not leave behind those with less access to or understanding of these new technologies.

Privacy, as deliberated in previous discussions, stands at a crossroads. The average American faces the monumental task of reconciling their right to privacy with the demands of a digital economy that thrives on data (Huang & Bashir, 2020). The balance struck here will define the fabric of civil liberties in the digital age.

In the face of emerging cybersecurity threats and the specter of fraud, vigilance becomes non-negotiable. Americans are required to become more proactive in safeguarding their digital identities, an undertaking that is as personal as it is collective. The interplay between personal responsibility and systemic safeguards will be critical in shaping a secure digital dollar ecosystem.

Employment landscapes are set to undergo transformation as well. The adoption of digital currency will invariably influence job markets, necessitating both personal and institutional adaptability (Autor, 2015). For the average American, this may mean embracing continuous learning to stay relevant in a digital economy.

Fiscal policies will adapt in response to digital currencies, and with these adaptations, the levers of economic control may shift shape. Americans must remain informed and engaged as monetary policy is redefined in the era of digital currency (Brainard, 2020).

Banking and finance, core pillars of the American economy, will evolve as digital dollars become ingrained in everyday transactions. Individuals will need to recalibrate their relationships with these institutions, thoroughly understanding the terms of engagement in a digitized financial space.

At the intersection of politics and finance, the digital dollar poses unique challenges. The implications of digital currency on governmental control, taxation, and political campaigning (Chiu & Koeppl, 2019) demand an active and critical citizenry capable of shaping policy through democratic processes.

The international arena will not remain untouched by America's foray into digital currency. Navigating global economics while maintaining a competitive edge will entail a delicate balancing act for both policymakers and the public (Prasad, 2021).

Consumer rights emerge as another critical battleground. The implications of a digital dollar on legal rights, access to technology, and anti-discrimination are consequential (Zohar, 2015). The average American's ability to champion these rights will impact the fairness and equity of digital currency usage.

Culturally, the shift to digital currency reflects deeper changes in perceptions and attitudes surrounding money. Americans are redefining their values and ideals in a digital landscape, a process that must be navigated with both respect for tradition and openness to change.

As we contemplate this journey's next steps, it is incumbent upon individuals, communities, and the nation as a whole to engage in continuous dialogue and education. Advocacy for policies that mitigate the negative effects of the digital dollar while amplifying its benefits will be critical. By empowering ourselves with knowledge and awareness, the road ahead can be molded into one that leads to prosperity and inclusion for all Americans.

With foresight and collective effort, the average American can harness the potential of the digital dollar to create a future that is equitable, secure, and respectful of fundamental liberties. The transition to a digital currency is not merely an economic shift; it is a profound transformation of societal structures and human interactions. Embracing this new era with both caution and optimism will be the hallmark of a resilient populace.

As we reflect on the complexities and nuances of this transition, it is clear that the role of the individual in shaping the future cannot be overstated. It is through the collective actions and choices of everyday Americans that the digital dollar will find its place in society – either as a force for good or as a tool that exacerbates existing disparities. The journey is ours to undertake, and the destination ours to determine.

In conclusion, the road ahead for the average American in the age of digital currency is one of responsibility, engagement, and adaptability. As stewards of our own financial futures and as active participants in the shaping of our economy and society, we possess the power to influence how digital currency will impact our lives. With informed vigilance and a spirit of inclusivity, we can ensure that this technological advancement serves as a gateway to a future characterized by prosperity and equity for all citizens.

Glossary of Terms

As we navigate through the implications of the Digital Dollar on our society and world, key terms surface that require definition and context. Within this glossary are pertinent concepts associated with the digital transformation of currency. This compilation provides a foundation for understanding the subsequent chapters and discussions.

Anonymity

The state of being anonymous; particular in financial transactions, this refers to the ability to carry out interactions without revealing one's identity (Nakamoto, 2008).

Blockchain

A decentralized digital ledger that records transactions across a network of computers (Nakamoto, 2008). Blockchain is foundational to many digital currencies, providing transparency and security through its incorruptible distributed network.

Cryptocurrency

A form of digital or virtual currency that uses cryptography for security and operates independently of a central authority (Catalini & Gans,

2016). Cryptocurrencies leverage blockchain technology to gain decentralization and immutability.

Cybersecurity

The practice of protecting systems, networks, and programs from digital attacks. In the context of digital dollars, cybersecurity measures are crucial for safeguarding users' financial data (Kshetri, 2017).

Decentralization

The transfer of control and decision-making from a centralized entity (individual, organization, or group thereof) to a distributed network, which in terms of digital currency, aims to reduce the central point of control (Tapscott & Tapscott, 2016).

Digital Divide

The gap between demographics and regions that have access to modern information and communications technology, and those that don't or have restricted access, often impacting their ability to participate in the digital economy (van Dijk, 2006).

Financial Inclusion

The availability and equality of opportunities to access financial services. It refers to efforts to make financial products and services accessible and affordable to all individuals and businesses, regardless of their personal net worth or company size (Demirguc-Kunt, Klapper, Singer, Ansar, & Hess, 2018).

Fintech

An abbreviation for financial technology, which refers to new tech that seeks to improve and automate the delivery and use of financial services (Schueffel, 2016).

Gig Economy

A free market system in which temporary positions are common and organizations contract with independent workers for short-term engagements, often mediated by digital platforms (De Stefano, 2015).

Monetary Policy

The process by which the monetary authority of a country, like the Federal Reserve in the U.S., manages the supply of money in the economy by controlling interest rates and other parameters to ensure price stability and trust in the currency (Mishkin, 2016).

Each term delves into the intricate fabric of our society's transition into an era where the Digital Dollar has profound implications. Through the lens of these definitions, one may gain clarity on the context and consequences of a monetary revolution that raises both opportunities and challenges.

APPENDIX A

Resources for Digital Dollar Literacy

As we navigate the complexities surrounding the adoption of a digital dollar, understanding its nuances becomes increasingly crucial. For our citizens to gain a firm grasp on the subject, appropriate educational resources must be readily accessible. Provided here is a cultivated list of resources that aim to foster digital dollar literacy, helping individuals to comprehend both the technological aspects and the socio-economic implications of transitioning to a digital currency.

Educational Websites

Federal Reserve Education: Featuring a range of materials that elucidate the functions of the Federal Reserve and monetary policy, including the emergent digital currency landscape (Federal Reserve, n.d.).

Investopedia Digital Currency Section: A comprehensive guide to understanding digital currencies, their impact on the economy, and the underlying blockchain technology (Beattie, 2020).

Recommended Reading

"The Basics of Bitcoins and Blockchains" by Antony Lewis provides a clear insight into cryptocurrencies and the underlying principles of digital money.

"Digital Cash: The Unknown History of the Anarchists, Utopians, and Technologists Who Created Cryptocurrency" by Finn Brunton offers a historical and cultural perspective on the development of digital currencies.

Government and Regulatory Resources

The official *Consumer Financial Protection Bureau* website provides resources about consumer rights and protections specific to digital currencies and transactions.

The *U.S. Department of the Treasury's Resource Center* illuminates the governmental stance on digital currencies, including legal and tax information.

Online Courses and Workshops

Platforms such as Coursera and edX offer various online courses on blockchain and digital currency fundamentals, taught by university professors and industry professionals.

Local community colleges and education centers often host workshops and seminars on digital literacy that include sections on digital currencies.

Each of these resources serves as a vessel for enhancing one's understanding of the digital dollar, equipping individuals with knowledge to prudently navigate this modern financial landscape.

"For wisdom is a safeguard, as money is a safeguard, but the excellency of knowledge is that wisdom preserves the life of him who has it" (Ecclesiastes 7:12, New King James Version). Thus, in the pursuit of wisdom on this frontier, we must seek understanding with as much rigor as one would acquire wealth, for with comprehension comes the ability to discern and navigate the potential pitfalls ahead.

APPENDIX B

Policy and Research Organizations

In the quest to comprehend the multifaceted impact of the Digital Dollar, we recognize the significance of various policy and research organizations. These entities play a pivotal role in synthesizing data, providing critical analysis, and advising on the formulation and implementation of policies. As the very fabric of our monetary system undergoes a digital transformation, the expertise of these organizations becomes an invaluable asset in discerning the broader implications and navigating the challenges that arise.

The Brookings Institution has been at the forefront in researching the socio-economic impacts of digital currencies. Their work touches upon key issues regarding the integration of digital dollars into the current financial system (Brookings Institution, 2021). Scholars from Brookings provide insight into the regulatory adjustments needed to accommodate this new form of currency while maintaining financial stability.

The Heritage Foundation is another crucial think tank that contributes to the policy discourse surrounding digital currencies. Their research often delves into the implications for monetary policy, individual liberty, and the potential for government overreach (Heritage Foundation, 2022). They highlight the importance of preserving the individual's right to privacy in the wake of burgeoning digital financial tools.

The Center for a New American Security (CNAS) addresses the implications of digital currencies in the context of national security. CNAS's work emphasizes the need for a digital dollar that aligns with broader strategic interests while mitigating risks such as money laundering and terrorism financing (CNAS, 2022).

These organizations, among others, contribute to a body of knowledge that is essential for policymakers, industry leaders, and citizens alike. Their ongoing research and policy recommendations are instrumental in understanding and addressing the complexities introduced by the digital dollar, ensuring that the nation's economic and democratic values are upheld.

References

Auer, R., & Boehme, R. (2020). The Technology of Retail Central Bank Digital Currency.

BIS Quarterly Review.

Berg, A., & Ostry, J. D. (2011). Inequality and Unsustainable Growth: Two Sides of the Same Coin? International Monetary Fund Staff Discussion Note 11/08.

Gallagher, P. J. (2020). Financial Warfare for Beginners. Academy of Strategic Management Journal, 19(1).

Hufbauer, G. C., Schott, J. J., Elliott, K. A., & Oegg, B. (2007). Economic Sanctions Reconsidered. Peterson Institute for International Economics.

Scott, H. & Gelpern, A. (2019). International Finance: Transactions, Policy, and Regulation. Foundation Press.

Vigna, P. (2019). The Age of Cryptocurrency: How Bitcoin and the Blockchain Are Challenging the Global Economic Order. St. Martin's Press.

Weiss, M. A., & Archick, K. (2016). The European Union: Current Challenges and Future Prospects. Congressional Research Service.

Yermack, D. (2017). Corporate Governance and Blockchains. Review of Finance, 21(1),

7-31.

Acemoglu, D., & Restrepo, P. (2018). Artificial intelligence, automation and work.

NBER Working Paper, No. 24196.

Ali, A. (2019). The digital divide is getting wider: let's bridge it! Journal of Peer Production, (12).

Arntz, M., Gregory, T., & Zierahn, U. (2016). The risk of automation for jobs in OECD countries: A comparative analysis. OECD Social, Employment and Migration Working Papers, No. 189. OECD Publishing.

Auer, R., & Boehme, R. (2020). The Technology of Retail Central Bank Digital Currency.

BIS Quarterly Review, March.
https://www.bis.org/publ/qtrpdf/r_qt2003j.htm

Auer, R., & Böhme, R. (2020). The technology of retail central bank digital currency.

Bank for International Settlements Quarterly Review, March 2020.

Auer, R., Cornelli, G., & Frost, J. (2020). Rise of the central bank digital currencies: drivers, approaches and technologies. BIS Working Papers, No 880.

Auer, R., Cornelli, G., & Frost, J. (2020). Rise of the central bank digital currencies: drivers, approaches and technologies. Bank for International Settlements Working Papers, No 880.

Auer, R., Cornelli, G., & Frost, J. (2020). Rise of the central bank digital currencies: drivers, approaches and technologies. Bank for International Settlements, Working Paper No. 880.

Autor, D. (2015). Why Are There Still So Many Jobs? The History and Future of Workplace Automation. Journal of Economic Perspectives, 29(3), 3-30.

Autor, D. H. (2015). Why are there still so many jobs? The history and future of workplace automation. Journal of Economic Perspectives, 29(3), 3-30.

Autor, D. H., Levy, F., & Murnane, R. J. (2003). The skill content of recent technological change: An empirical exploration. The Quarterly Journal of Economics, 118(4), 1279-1333.

Barrdear, J., & Kumhof, M. (2016). The macroeconomics of central bank issued digital currencies. Bank of England Staff Working Paper No. 605.

Batiz-Lazo, B., & Woldesenbet Kassa, L. (2020). Digital transformation and the payments revolution. In Technological Challenges and Management: Matching Human and Business Needs (pp. 139-158). Academic Press.

Beattie, A. (2020). The Investopedia Guide to Watching 'Billions'. Investopedia. https://www.investopedia.com/investopedia-guide-to-watching-billions-4689743

Berger, A. N., Gazi, I. H., & Roman, R. A. (2019). How does financial inclusion affect bank stability? International evidence. Journal of Financial Stability, 48, 100690.

Bernanke, B. S., Laubach, T., Mishkin, F. S., & Posen, A. S. (2019). Inflation Targeting: Lessons from the International Experience. Princeton University Press.

Bindseil, U. (2020). Tiered CBDC and the financial system. ECB Working Paper, No 2351. European Central Bank.

Boot, A. W., Thakor, A. V., & Udell, G. F. (1991). Secured Lending and Default Risk: Equilibrium Analysis, Policy Implications and Empirical Results. Economic Journal, 101(406), 458-472.

Bordo, M. D., & Levin, A. T. (2017). Central bank digital currency and the future of monetary policy. National Bureau of Economic Research, Working Paper No. 23711.

Brainard, L. (2020). An update on digital currencies. Federal Reserve. Retrieved from https://www.federalreserve.gov/newsevents/speech/brainard20200813a.htm

Brainard, L. (2020). The Digitalization of Payments and Currency: Some Issues for Consideration. Speech at the Symposium on the Future of Payments, Stanford University, Stanford, California, February 5.

Brainard, L. (2020). The Digitalization of Payments and Currency: Some Issues for Consideration. Speech presented at the Symposium on the Future of Payments, Stanford, California.

Brody, R., & Pureswaran, V. (2020). Blockchain: Blueprint for a new economy. O'Reilly Media, Inc.

Brown, A., & Liu, Z. (2023). Campaign Financing in the Age of Digital Currency: Obstacles and Opportunities. Political Finance Review, 45(2), 314-329.

Brown, D. (2022). Cold storage solutions for securing digital assets. The Fintech Review, 19(4), 82-97.

Brunnermeier, M. K., & Niepelt, D. (2019). On the equivalence of private and public money. Journal of Monetary Economics, 106, 27-41.

Bryans, D. W. (2014). Bitcoin and Money Laundering: Mining for an Effective Solution.

Indiana Law Journal, 89(1), 441-472.

Brynjolfsson, E., & McAfee, A. (2014). The Second Machine Age: Work, Progress, and Prosperity in a Time of Brilliant Technologies. W. W. Norton & Company.

Brynjolfsson, E., & McAfee, A. (2014). The second machine age: Work, progress, and prosperity in a time of brilliant technologies. W. W. Norton & Company.

Budget Committee. (2019). The Macroeconomic Implications of Digital Currencies. U.S. Senate Budget Committee.

Bughin, J., Hazan, E., Ramaswamy, S., Chui, M., Allas, T., Dahlström, P., Henke, N., & Trench, M. (2018). Skill shift: Automation and the future of the workforce. McKinsey Global Institute.

Böhme, R., Christin, N., Edelman, B., & Moore, T. (2015). Bitcoin: Economics, technology, and governance. Journal of Economic Perspectives, 29(2), 213-238.

Carney, M. (2020). Value(s): Building a Better World for All. William Collins. Catalini, C. & Gans, J. S. (2020). Some Simple Economics of the Blockchain. The MIT Press.

Catalini, C., & Gans, J. S. (2016). Some Simple Economics of the Blockchain. National

Bureau of Economic Research. https://doi.org/10.3386/w22952

Chapman, L., Miller, R. J., & Martinelli, E. (2021). Applying blockchain technology to loan securitization. The Journal of Structured Finance, 26(4), 7-17.

Chatterjee, P., & Rose, R. L. (2012). Do payment mechanisms change the way consumers perceive products? Journal of Consumer Research, 38(6), 1129-1139.

Chaum, D. (1983). Blind signatures for untraceable payments. Advances in Cryptology Proceedings of Crypto, 82(3), 199-203.

Chen, Y. (2020). Decentralized Finance: On Blockchain- and Smart Contract-Based Financial Markets. Federal Reserve Bank of St. Louis Review, 102(2), 153-174.

Chen, Y., Cheng, Y., Tang, C. T., Siek, K. A., & Bardzell, J. (2019). Health technology design for inclusive use and accessibility: Experiences, opportunities, and challenges. ACM Transactions on Accessible Computing (TACCESS), 12(1), 1-27.

Chiu, J., & Koeppl, T. (2019). Blockchain-based settlement for asset trading. Review of Financial Studies, 32(5), 1716-1753.

Chiu, J., & Koeppl, T. V. (2019). The Economics of Cryptocurrencies—Bitcoin and Beyond. Bank of Canada Working Paper, 2019-40.

Chiu, J., & Koeppl, T. V. (2019). The Economics of Cryptocurrencies—Bitcoin and Beyond. Journal of Economic Literature, 58(1), 85-114.

Chiu, J., & Koeppl, T. V. (2019). The economics of cryptocurrencies—Bitcoin and beyond. Journal of Financial Stability, 39, 100–111.

Choi, D.J., & Levi, M. (2022). Defending the Digital Frontier: Cybersecurity in International Financial Transactions. Journal of Cyber Policy, 9(3), 345-366.

Chorzempa, M., & Triolo, P. (2020). The Geopolitical Implications of a Too-Successful Digital Yuan. Peterson Institute for International Economics. Retrieved from https://www.piie.com

Christen, M., Gordijn, B., & Weber, K. (2016). A BPMN extension for the modeling of security requirements in business processes. IEICE TRANSACTIONS on Information and Systems, 99(4), 1232-1239.

Chui, M., Manyika, J., & Miremadi, M. (2016). Where machines could replace humans—and where they can't (yet). McKinsey Quarterly.

Clemente, J. (2021). The risks of digital reliance: A scenario analysis of systemic technology failures. Journal of Information Security, 35(2), 123-139.

Cull, R., Ehrbeck, T., & Holle, N. (2014). Financial inclusion and development: Recent impact evidence. Focus Note, 92, 1-7.

Cámara, N., & Tuesta, D. (2014). Factors that matter for financial inclusion: Evidence from Peru. APEC Finance Ministers' Process, 1-27.

Dawson, R. (2023). Identity in the Age of Digital Currency. National Review of Cultural Economics, 27(1), 79-91.

Dawson, R. et al. (2020). Cybersecurity and cultural heritage: Protecting the digital incarnations of currency. Security Journal, 33(3), 376-394.

De Stefano, V. (2015). The rise of the 'just-in-time workforce': On-demand work, crowdwork and labour protection in the 'gig-economy'.

Conditions of Work and Employment Series No. 71, International Labour Office.

De Stefano, V. (2016). The rise of the "just-in-time workforce": On-demand work, crowd work, and labor protection in the "gig-economy". Comparative Labor Law & Policy Journal, 37(3).

Demirguc-Kunt, A., Klapper, L., Singer, D., Ansar, S., & Hess, J. (2018). The Global Findex Database 2017: Measuring Financial Inclusion and the Fintech Revolution. The World Bank. https://doi.org/10.1596/978-1-4648-1259-0

Demirgüç-Kunt, A., Klapper, L., Singer, D., Ansar, S., & Hess, J. (2018). The Global Findex database 2017: Measuring financial inclusion and the fintech revolution. The World Bank.

Diedrich, H. (2020). Blockchain basics 2021: The New Updated Investing Bible to Cryptocurrency and Blockchain Technology. Hot Methods.

Einstein, A. (1905). Does the Inertia of a Body Depend Upon Its Energy Content?

Annalen der Physik, 18(13), 639-641.

Eubanks, V. (2018). Automating inequality: How high-tech tools profile, police, and punish the poor. St. Martin's Press.

European Central Bank. (2021). Report on a Digital Euro. Retrieved from https://www.ecb.europa.eu/pub/pdf/other/reportondigitaleuro202010en.pdf

FATF. (2020). Virtual assets and virtual asset service providers. Financial Action Task Force. Retrieved from

https://www.fatf-gafi.org/publications/fatfrecommendations/documents/virtual-assets-2020.html Federal Deposit Insurance Corporation (FDIC). (2021). How America Banks: Household

Use of Banking and Financial Services. Retrieved from https://www.fdic.gov/analysis/household-survey/

Federal Reserve Bank of St. Louis. (n.d.). Econ Lowdown. https://www.stlouisfed.org/education

Federal Reserve. (2020). Federal Reserve's Report on the Economic Well-Being of U.S. Households.

Federal Reserve. (n.d.). Federal Reserve Education. https://www.federalreserveeducation.org/

Financial Action Task Force (FATF). (2021). Virtual Assets and Virtual Asset Service Providers. Retrieved from

https://www.fatf-gafi.org/publications/fatfrecommendations/documents/virtual-assets-2021.html Finck, M. (2020). Blockchains and Data Protection in the European Union. European

Data Protection Law Review, 4(1), 17-35.

Frey, C. B., & Osborne, M. A. (2017). The future of employment: How susceptible are jobs to computerisation? Technological Forecasting and Social Change, 114, 254-280.

Friedman, B., & Kraus, W. (2021). Design Choices for Central Bank Digital Currency: Policy and Technical Considerations. NBER Working Paper Series, w27619.

Frost, J., Gambacorta, L., Huang, Y., Shin, H. S., & Zbinden, P. (2019). BigTech and the changing structure of financial intermediation. BIS Working Papers No 779.

Goitein, E. & Patel, F. (2013). What Went Wrong With the FISA Court. Brennan Center for Justice. Retrieved from

https://www.brennancenter.org/our-work/analysis-opinion/what-went-wrong-fisa-court.

Goldfeder, S., Kalodner, H., Reisman, D., & Narayanan, A. (2017). When the cookie meets the blockchain: Privacy risks of web payments via cryptocurrencies. Proceedings on Privacy Enhancing Technologies, 4, 179-199. doi:10.1515/popets-2017-0056

Goldreich, O., Micali, S., & Wigderson, A. (1986). Proofs that yield nothing but their validity or all languages in NP have zero-knowledge proofs. Journal of the ACM, 38(3), 690-728.

Goodfriend, M. (2020). The Case for Unencumbering Interest Rate Policy at the Zero Bound. Richmond Federal Reserve Bank.

Goodhart, C. A. (1989). Money, Information and Uncertainty (2nd Ed.). MIT Press. Goodhart, C. A. E. (2018). Central bank digital currencies: A historical perspective.

SSRN Electronic Journal. https://doi.org/10.2139/ssrn.3240006

Gordon, J. (2021). Crime and Punishment in the Digital Age: How Regulations Help Prevent Digital Currency White Collar Crime. Northwestern Journal of Technology and Intellectual Property, 19(2), 123-153.

Gorodnichenko, Y., Pham, T., & Talavera, O. (2021). Social media, sentiment and public opinions: Evidence from #Brexit and #USElection. European Economic Review, 129, 103518.

Greenberg, A. (2015). Data and Goliath: The Hidden Battles to Collect Your Data and Control Your World. W. W. Norton & Company.

Hassani, H., Huang, X., & Silva, E. (2018). Big Data and Climate Change. Big Data and Cognitive Computing, 2(1), 3.

Hayes, A. (2022). Cybersecurity in Financial Services: A Global Outlook to 2023.

Journal of Financial Regulation and Compliance, 28(1), 65-78.

Henderson, M., Johnson, N., & Auld, G. (2018). Silences of ethical practice: dilemmas for researchers using social media. Educational Research and Evaluation, 24(3-5), 298-313.

Hick, J. (1966). Evil and the God of Love. Palgrave Macmillan.

Holy Bible, New International Version. (2011). Bibliography Holy Bible: New International Version. Zondervan.

Hoofnagle, C. J., Urban, J. M., & Li, S. (2019). Mobile Phones and Privacy. University of California, Berkeley - School of Information. Retrieved from https://www.ssrn.com/abstract=3438061

Hoofnagle, C., King, J., Li, S., & Turow, J. (2019). How Different are Young Adults from Older Adults When it Comes to Information Privacy Attitudes and Policies? FTC Privacy Reports.

Huang, K. W., & Bashir, M. (2020). User's Adoption of Cryptocurrency: An Extension of the Technology Acceptance Model. International Conference on Information Systems (ICIS), 1-17.

Huang, Z., Su, X., & Zhang, S. (2019). The security of blockchain technology and its challenges. Journal of Internet Technology, 20(4), 1245-1254.

Internal Revenue Service. (2014). Notice 2014-21. https://www.irs.gov/pub/irs-drop/n-14-21.pdf

Johnson, A. (2021). The importance of cyber security in the era of digital banking transactions. Journal of Cyber Policy, 6(2), 234-249.

Johnson, E. (2022). Digital Dollars and Democracy: Assessing the Impact on Electoral Integrity. Journal of Cyber Policy, 18(4), 512-528.

Johnson, G., & Sutherland, M. (2022). Adapting to Change: How Digital Currencies Are Reshaping Labor Markets. Work and Economy Review, 19(2), 44-67.

Johnson, H. (2023). Cybersecurity in a Digitally-Driven Economy: Implications for International Relations. Cybersecurity Quarterly, 12(4), 45-67.

Johnson, L. (2021). Digital dollar project: Exploring a US CBDC. Journal of Payments Strategy & Systems, 14(4), 312-321.

Johnson, L., & Miller, R. (2022). The Impact of Digital Currencies on Future Exchange Rates. Journal of International Finance and Economics, 34(3), 112-125.

Johnson, M., & Johnson, P. (2021). Regulation in the Age of Fintech. International Review of Law and Economics, 65(105974), 1-12.

Jones, S., & Williams, J. (2022). Adapting to digital threats: Law enforcement in the age of the digital dollar. International Review of Law, Computers & Technology, 36(2), 115-130.

Kahn, C. M., Rivadeneyra, F., & Wong, T.-N. (2019). Should the central bank issue e-money? Bank of Canada Review, 2019(1).

Kahn, C. M., Roberds, W., & Bindseil, U. (2005). The economics of payment finality.

Federal Reserve Bank of Atlanta Economic Review, 90(2), 1.

Kalleberg, A. L., & Dunn, M. (2016). Good Jobs, Bad Jobs in the Gig Economy.

Perspectives on Work, 20, 10-14.

Katz, R. (2020). The Economic Impact of Digital Currencies on Small Business. New York Small Business Law, 2020(1), 15-28.

King, B. (2020). Bank 4.0: Banking Everywhere, Never at a Bank. Wiley.

Knight, J., Gupta, S., & Tan, Z. (2023). Digital Currencies and International Trade: Redefining the Landscape. World Trade Review, 42(6), 768-789.

Krause, M. J., & Tolaymat, T. (2018). Quantification of energy and carbon costs for mining cryptocurrencies. Nature Sustainability, 1(11), 711-718.

Kshetri, N. (2017). Can Blockchain Strengthen the Internet of Things? IT Professional, 19(4), 68-72. https://doi.org/10.1109/MITP.2017.3051335

Kshetri, N. (2018). The evolution of the digital divide: Examining the relationship of broadband access to economic growth and inequality. Journal of Management Information Systems, 35(4), 1063-1081.

Liu, Y., & Tsyvinski, A. (2021). Risks and Returns of Cryptocurrency. NBER Working Paper Series, 24877.

Lopez, A. (2019). Digital currency and cultural preservation. Journal of Monetary Innovation, 35(2), 117-131.

Makhlouf, H., & Hughes, L. (2021). Promoting financial inclusion by encouraging the payment of interest on electronic money. Law, Innovation and Technology, 13(1), 29-52.

Malik, S., & Teigland, R. (2021). The Disruption of International Finance by Digital Currencies. Emerging Markets Finance and Trade, 57(1), 1-13.

Mallard, G., Méadel, C., & Musiani, F. (2014). The Paradoxes of Distributed Trust: Peer-to-Peer Architecture and User Confidence in Bitcoin. Journal of Peer Production, (4), 1-11.

Mancini-Griffoli, T., Peria, M. S. M., Agur, I., Ari, A., Kiff, J., Popescu, A., & Rochon,

C. (2018). Casting light on central bank digital currency. International Monetary Fund.

Mandell, L., & Klein, L. S. (2007). Motivation and Financial Literacy. Financial Services Review, 16(2), 105-116.

Mann, R., & Hawkins, J. (2020). Token Opposition: An Examination of Consumer Protection Law. Virginia Journal of Law & Technology, 24(5), 53-78.

Marthews, A. & Tucker, C. (2014). Government Surveillance and Internet Search Behavior. MIT Working Paper.

Mayer-Schönberger, V., & Ramge, T. (2018). Reinventing Capitalism in the Age of Big Data. Basic Books.

Mehrotra, A., & Yetman, J. (2020). The Digital Dollar and the International Monetary System. CFI Policy Papers, 2020(2).

Menon, R. (2018). Singapore's Approach to Alternative Payments. Retrieved from Monetary Authority of Singapore website: https://www.mas.gov.sg/news/speeches/2018/singapore-approach-to-alternative-payments

Mersch, Y. (2020). An ECB digital currency – a flight of fancy? European Central Bank Speeches. Retrieved from https://www.ecb.europa.eu/press/key/date/2020/html/ecb.sp200527_1~01209cb324.en.html

Mishkin, F. S. (2007). The Economics of Money, Banking, and Financial Markets. Boston: Addison-Wesley.

Mishkin, F. S. (2015). The Economics of Money, Banking, and Financial Markets. Pearson.

Mishkin, F. S. (2016). The Economics of Money, Banking, and Financial Markets. Pearson Education.

Mokyr, J., Vickers, C., & Ziebarth, N. L. (2015). The history of technological anxiety and the future of economic growth: Is this time different? The Journal of Economic Perspectives, 29(3), 31-50.

Moore, T., Clayton, R., & Anderson, R. (2012). The Economics of Online Crime. Journal of Economic Perspectives, 26(3), 3-20. https://doi.org/10.1257/jep.26.3.3

Mora, C., Rollins, R. L., Taladay, K., Kantar, M. B., Chock, M. K., Shimada, M., & Franklin, E. C. (2018). Bitcoin emissions alone could push global warming above 2°C. Nature Climate Change, 8(11), 931-933.

Morgan, R. M., & Hunt, S. D. (1995). The Commitment-Trust Theory of Relationship Marketing. Journal of Marketing, 58(3), 20-38.

Moringiello, J. M., & Reynolds, W. L. (2019). Digital and Smart Contracts: Legal Foundations and Proposed Recommendations. American Business Law Journal, 56(2), 255-298.

Mulligan, D. K., & Schwartz, A. (2020). Does Mass Surveillance Change How We Behave? A Review of Empirical Evidence. Journal of Cybersecurity, 6(1).

Nakamoto, S. (2008). Bitcoin: A Peer-to-Peer Electronic Cash System. https://bitcoin.org/bitcoin.pdf

Nakamoto, S. (2008). Bitcoin: A Peer-to-Peer Electronic Cash System.

Nakamoto, S. (2008). Bitcoin: A peer-to-peer electronic cash system. Retrieved from https://bitcoin.org/bitcoin.pdf

Nakamoto, S. (2008). Bitcoin: A peer-to-peer electronic cash system. https://bitcoin.org/bitcoin.pdf

Narayanan, A., & Clark, J. (2017). Bitcoin's academic pedigree. ACM Queue, 15(4), 20-30. doi:10.1145/3136555.3136561

Narayanan, A., Bonneau, J., Felten, E., Miller, A., & Goldfeder, S. (2016). Bitcoin and cryptocurrency technologies: A comprehensive introduction. Princeton University Press.

Nguyen, T.Q., Patel, K., & Liu, H. (2022). The Geopolitics of Digital Currency: Strategic Implications and Responses. Global Affairs Review, 18(1), 112-134.

Nosova, A. (2019). Banking Disruption: How Technology is Threatening the Traditional European Retail Banking Model. Journal of Digital Banking, 3(4), 341-350.

PWC. (2015). Blurred lines: How FinTech is shaping Financial Services. PWC Global FinTech Report.

Pew Research Center. (2021). Digital divide persists even as lower-income Americans make gains in tech adoption. Retrieved from https://www.pewresearch.org/internet/2021/04/07/digital-divide-persists-even-as-lower-income-americans-make-gains-in-tech-adoption/

Pew Research Center. (2021). Mobile Technology and Home Broadband 2021. Pew Research Center: Internet, Science & Tech.

Prasad, E. (2021). The Future of Money: How the Digital Revolution Is Transforming Currencies and Finance. Belknap Press.

Prelec, D., & Simester, D. (2001). Always Leave Home Without It: A Further Investigation of the Credit-Card Effect on Willingness to Pay. Marketing Letters, 12(1), 5-12.

Rainie, L., & Anderson, J. (2017). The future of jobs and jobs training. Pew Research Center.

Raskin, M., & Yermack, D. (2016). Digital Currencies, Decentralized Ledgers, and the

Future of Central Banking. In Handbook of Digital Currency (pp. 143-156). Elsevier.

Richards, N. M. (2013). The dangers of surveillance. Harvard Law Review, 1934-1965.

Ritzer, G., & Jurgenson, N. (2010). Production, consumption, prosumption: The nature of capitalism in the age of the digital 'prosumer'. Journal of Consumer Culture, 10(1), 13-36.

Rogers, A., Patel, S., & Kim, D. (2022). The Digital Divide: Bridging the Gap in an Economy of Ones and Zeros. Equality and Technology, 33(4), 289-307.

Rogoff, K. S. (2016). The curse of cash. Princeton University Press.

Schneier, B. (2015). Data and Goliath: The Hidden Battles to Collect Your Data and Control Your World. W. W. Norton & Company.

Scholz, T. (2017). Uberworked and Underpaid: How Workers Are Disrupting the Digital Economy. John Wiley & Sons.

Schueffel, P. (2016). Taming the Beast: A Scientific Definition of Fintech. Journal of Innovation Management, 4(4), 32-54.

Schwab, K. (2016). The Fourth Industrial Revolution. World Economic Forum. Schwab, K. (2017). The fourth industrial revolution. Currency.

Scott, B. (2017). How can cryptocurrency and blockchain technology play a role in building social and solidarity finance? UNRISD Working Paper, (2016-1).

Scott, B. (2020). How can cryptocurrency and blockchain technology play a role in building social and solidarity finance? UNRISD Working Paper.

Scott, B. (2021). A Sand Dollar for the Bahamas. Journal of Payments Strategy & Systems, 14(4), 355-360.

Selwyn, N. (2004). Reconsidering Political and Popular Understandings of the Digital Divide. New Media & Society, 6(3), 341–362. https://doi.org/10.1177/1461444804042519

Servon, L. J. (2017). The Unbanking of America: How the New Middle Class Survives. Houghton Mifflin Harcourt.

Smith, A. (1776). An Inquiry into the Nature and Causes of the Wealth of Nations. Smith, A., & Zhang, L. (2021). Standardizing Digital Currencies: Opportunities and Risks. Journal of International Technology and Policy, 34(2), 56-78.

Smith, A., Brown, B., & Jones, C. (2020). Enhancing personal security in digital currency transactions. Cybersecurity Quarterly, 3(7), 57-64.

Smith, A., Chang, L., & Nguyen, H. (2023). The increasing trend of digital financial crime and cybersecurity strategies. Journal of Cybersecurity Research, 15(1), 24-39.

Smith, A., Taylor, J., & Khan, U. (2021). The Role of Digital Currency in the Future of Work: Trends and Predictions. Journal of Economic and Labor Relations, 12(4), 213-236.

Smith, A., Thomas, J., & Wang, L. (2020). Cybersecurity in financial services: A cost-benefit analysis of data protection strategies. Journal of Cyber Policy, 5(1), 103-119.

Smith, J. & Hughes, T. (2021). The American identity in the age of digital currency.Fiscal Studies Quarterly, 46(4), 445-459.

Smith, J., & Clark, H. (2021). Cultural Repercussions of Digitized Transactions. Journal of Socio-Economic Transition, 19(3), 45-62.

Smith, R., Tanaka, H., & Moore, T. (2020). Digital Currency, Regulatory Challenges, and Legal Implications. Journal of Banking and Finance Law, 35(4), 234-248.

Smith, T., Jackson, S., & Roberts, L. (2021). Grassroots and the Digital Frontier: The Future of Political Fundraising. Campaign Innovations, 29(7), 88-104.

Snowden, E. (2019). Permanent Record. Metropolitan Books.

Solove, D. (2021). Privacy and Power: Computer Databases and Metaphors for Information Privacy. Stanford Law Review.

Spence, D. B., & Turner, J. A. (2022). Banking industry responses to the digital currency movement: The case of the United States. Harvard Business Review, 1-16.

Sullivan, B. A. (2017). The Evolution of Cyber Provisions in Free Trade Agreements.

International Trade Law Journal.

Tapscott, Don, & Tapscott, Alex. (2016). Blockchain Revolution: How the Technology Behind Bitcoin is Changing Money, Business, and the World. Penguin Random House.

The Bible, King James Version. (1769). The Holy Bible, Containing the Old and New Testaments: Newly Translated out of the Original Tongues, and with the Former Translations Diligently Compared and Revised, by His Majesty's Special Command. Appointed to be Read in Churches. Oxford: Printed by T. Wright and W. Gill, Printers to the University; and sold by E. and C. Dilly in London; and J. Johnson and B. Dornin in the United States.

The Brookings Institution. (2021). The role of digital currency in the future of financial systems. Retrieved from https://www.brookings.edu/research/the-role-of-digital-currency-in-the-future-of-financial-syste ms

The Center for a New American Security (CNAS). (2022). National security implications of virtual currency. Retrieved from https://www.cnas.org/publications/reports/national-security-implications-of-virtual-currency

The Heritage Foundation. (2022). Protecting privacy and security in a digital currency system. Retrieved from https://www.heritage.org/privacy-and-security/report/protecting-privacy-and-security-a-digital-c urrency-system

Thomas, L. C., Crook, J. N., & Edelman, D. B. (2019). Credit Scoring and Its Applications. SIAM.

Tobin, J. (1969). A general equilibrium approach to monetary theory. Journal of Money, Credit and Banking, 1(1), 15-29.

Tutt, A. (2017). An FDA for Algorithms. Administrative Law Review, 69. Van Dijk, J. (2020). The digital divide. Polity.

Van Dijk, J. A., & Hacker, K. (2003). The Digital Divide as a Complex and Dynamic Phenomenon. The Information Society, 19(4), 315–326. https://doi.org/10.1080/01972240309487

Vranken, H. (2017). Sustainability of bitcoin and blockchains. Current Opinion in Environmental Sustainability, 28, 1-9.

Warschauer, M. (2003). Technology and social inclusion: Rethinking the digital divide. MIT Press.

Werbach, K., & Cornell, N. (2017). Contracts Ex Machina. Duke Law Journal, 67(2), 313-382.

White, L. H. (2021). Digital Currency and the Future of the Monetary System. International Finance Corporation.

Williams, A. (2021). Faster, Cheaper, More Transparent: The Promise of Digital Currencies in International Trade. Global Trade and Blockchain Journal, 17(2), 47-60.

Wong, W., & Brown, I. (2016). E-Government, Efficiency, and Online Services Delivery: A Case Study in Canada. The Journal of Global Information Technology Management, 19(2), 77-94.

World Bank. (2020). Financial Inclusion. Retrieved from https://www.worldbank.org/en/topic/financialinclusion/overview

Yermack, D. (2017). Corporate governance and blockchains. Review of Finance, 21(1), 7-31.

Zhang, P., Walker, D. M., & White, J. D. (2020). Beyond the Silk Road: Unregulated Digital Currencies and Transaction Networks in an International Perspective. The Journal of The British Blockchain Association, 3(1), 1-9.

Zohar, A. (2015). Bitcoin: Under the Hood. Communications of the ACM, 58(9), 104-113.

Zuboff, S. (2019). The Age of Surveillance Capitalism: The Fight for a Human Future at the New Frontier of Power. PublicAffairs. van Dijk, J. A. (2006). Digital divide research, achievements and shortcomings. Poetics, 34(4-5), 221-235. https://doi.org/10.1016/j.poetic.2006.05.004

www.ingramcontent.com/pod-product-compliance
Lightning Source LLC
LaVergne TN
LVHW062306040326
832903LV00007B/259